THE ULTIMATE GUIDE TO DIVINATION

THE BEGINNER'S GUIDE TO USING CARDS, CRYSTALS, RUNES, PALMISTRY, AND MORE FOR INSIGHT AND PREDICTING THE FUTURE

LIZ DEAN

FAIR WINDS

Inspiring | Educating | Creating | Entertaining

Brimming with creative inspiration, how-to projects, and useful information to enrich your everyday life, Quarto Knows is a favorite destination for those pursuing their interests and passions. Visit our site and dig deeper with our books into your area of interest: Quarto Creates, Quarto Cooks, Quarto Homes, Quarto Lives, Quarto Drives, Quarto Explores, Quarto Gifts, or Quarto Kids.

© 2018 Quarto Publishing Group USA Inc.
Text © 2018 Liz Dean

First Published in 2018 by Fair Winds Press, an imprint of The Quarto Group, 100 Cummings Center, Suite 265-D, Beverly, MA 01915, USA.
T (978) 282-9590 F (978) 283-2742 QuartoKnows.com

Fair Winds Press titles are also available at discount for retail, wholesale, promotional, and bulk purchase. For details, contact the Special Sales Manager by email at specialsales@quarto.com or by mail at The Quarto Group, Attn: Special Sales Manager, 401 Second Avenue North, Suite 310, Minneapolis, MN 55401, USA.

22 21 20 19 18   1 2 3 4 5

ISBN: 978-1-59233-778-1

Library of Congress Cataloging-in-Publication Data is available

Illustrations from the Radiant Rider-Waite Tarot Deck® reproduced by permission of U.S. Games Systems, Inc., Stamford, CT 06902 USA. Copyright © 2006 by U.S. Games Systems, Inc. Further reproduction prohibited. The Radiant Rider-Waite Tarot Deck® is a registered trademark of U.S. Games Systems, Inc.

Cover Design: Debbie Berne
Cover Illustration: Mattie Wells
Page Layout: Mattie Wells
Photography: Shutterstock on pages 15, 19, 20, 27–39, 43, 122, 123, 136–143
Illustration: Mattie Wells

Printed in China

"What you seek is seeking you."
—Rumi

CONTENTS

1 INTRODUCING DIVINATION

If you have this book in your hands, you are answering a call to connect with your intuitive wisdom; it's time to explore, find, or reconnect with a divinatory art that resonates with you. This book presents the key tools and techniques for divination: crystal casting and pendulums; runes; teacup, coffee cup, and salt readings; palmistry; playing cards and tarot cards; numerology; dice reading; and crystal ball gazing. These art forms gave our ancestors answers, and they will give you, too, special insights into the past, present, and future.

While it's impossible to cover each one in depth here, I hope that you are inspired to try new practices and gain new insights into those with which you are familiar.

HOW DIVINATION WORKS

Divination, from the Latin *divinare* ("to foresee"), is to connect with the divine; it's a ritual means of accessing hidden knowledge. The divine can be thought of both as an external intelligence (the Universe, Source, God, angels, or beings in spirit) and as the divinity within each of us—our innate wisdom, or inner knowing. We are all connected; divination potentially puts us in touch with collective wisdom—what Carl Jung called the collective unconscious.

Divination gives us a set of rituals through which we shift from logic to intuition, ways to tune in to this unconscious wisdom to help us find the answers we seek. When we are laying out cards, making a pot of tea, or adding up numbers for a numerology reading, the logical left brain is distracted with a task; it's believed that this distraction allows us to connect more deeply with the intuitive right brain. With the left brain not intercepting or judging our intuitive, sensory messages, we begin to experience a different

A NOTE ABOUT THE FUTURE

If you are dipping into divination for the first time, it's important to understand what is meant by future or outcome. This is the most likely outcome given present circumstances—which change constantly. A reading suggests the potential future at the time of the reading; the future is not fixed. We have free will, and as we change, so can the future.

kind of knowing, a new quality of awareness. We shift into intuition, or "reading" mode, through which we experience our own truth.

HOW DIVINATION CAN **BENEFIT YOU**

Divination tools can offer you much more than an answer to a question. Although a question is where we all begin, working regularly with your crystals, cards, runes, or teacups offers a more precious gift: time with yourself to explore in detail any aspect of your life path. This leads to greater self-awareness, empowerment, and purpose. You'll become more sensitive to your own and others' needs, and you'll be more attuned to the energies around you—physically and spiritually. Divination also supports creativity, as you look at options, try on new scenarios, and see new pathways.

Practice divination regularly, and you can gain more self-trust, seeing the value in your ideas and insights. It's helpful to keep a divination diary, if you can; take notes after your readings, add the date, and reflect on them in the future.

ASKING QUESTIONS FOR DIVINATION

Before you begin with any divination technique, formulate your question. If the question is right, the answer is more likely to make sense to you. In my work as a tarot teacher and reader, I help people formulate questions that really reflect their situations. The most common request is, "Will he or she come back?" My response is, "Is this really the question?" Most people already know the answer. What they're really seeking is confirmation, and confirmation requires a yes-no response. In divination, it's best to avoid these closed questions (unless you do want a yes-or-no answer and if so, try working with a pendulum; see page 26). They set a limit on a reading, narrowing it to one answer rather than exploring the myriad possibilities a good reading can offer. Instead, the questioner might ask, "What can make me happy?" or "What do I need to know now?" The answer to their original question will usually arise within the scope of a much broader, more rewarding reading.

2 ORACLES OF THE ANCIENTS

CRYSTAL, STONE, AND WOOD

To foretell the future, our ancestors turned to the natural resources of their environments—harvesting small stones and crystals from the earth or carving runic symbols on stone and wood. They sought counsel on whether they would survive battle, illness, or a dangerous voyage or if their herd or a marriage would bring prosperity. From them, we have inherited some of the simplest yet most powerful techniques for divination. In this chapter, you'll see how to divine with crystals, cast runes, and use a pendulum.

DIVINATION
WITH
CRYSTALS

Divining with stones was practiced at the Temple of Apollo at Delphi, the famous oracle site built around the seventh century BCE. The Homeric Hymns, a collection of poems to Greek deities dating from the same era, refers to the Thriae, three-winged sisters credited with inventing fortune-telling by means of little stones: mantic, or prophecy, stones placed on a dish would move in answer to a question.

On Tsaghkahovit Plain in central Armenia, researchers discovered a three-thousand-year-old settlement—and evidence of divination by lithomancy (the use of bones and stones). One shrine included eighteen pebbles that appear to have been used for divination. The researchers also unearthed other divination tools: marked animal knuckle bones and dough stamped with symbols. Although it had lasted for around one hundred years, the settlement had been suddenly abandoned, leaving researchers wondering if the diviners had predicted the likely end of their own lives if they had stayed.

Today, the shamans of Tuva in southern Siberia still follow the tradition of fortune-telling with stones. Each divination stone is collected from a different river and is believed to hold the river's wisdom. This suggests that the provenance of the stones and crystals we use for divination is important.

When you intentionally seek stones, you are setting the intention for powerful and helpful divination. Some crystals, however, find you. You might come across a stone on a walk, be given a crystal by someone important to you, or be drawn to a crystal in a shop. Each crystal makes a journey toward you.

PREPARING FOR A CRYSTAL READING

In a reading, we interpret a group of chosen crystals that fall randomly or are placed in a layout. Interpreting the random fall of crystals is known as stone-casting.

You will need a selection of crystals and a reading mat. Professional crystal readers may have around forty or fifty small crystals from which nine or ten are chosen for a reading. The crystals listed in this book include many that are commonly used in healing and divination, but this list isn't exclusive; collect and use crystals that you feel a connection with. Keep your crystals wrapped in fabric, such as silk, in a soft bag or purse to protect them physically and energetically when they are not being used.

You can make a mat on which to cast, or gently throw, your crystals by folding a cloth or scarf into an approximate square. Make sure that it is thick enough to protect the crystals when they fall and release them gently, not too high over the mat, to ensure that any more fragile pieces do not become damaged (some crystals, such as selenite, can flake or break easily). The mat is an important part of the reading because we interpret the positions of the stones on (and off) it, so it is worthwhile to create one that reflects the special ritual of casting stones. For example, you might choose material of a color that helps you feel calm and self-connected, such as blue or purple, rather than a color that shouts for attention.

15

If you do not have many crystals in your collection, you can use a pendulum over the crystal directory (see page 39) to get a divinatory message right now.

Purple Fluorite

Jade

Amber

Rose Quartz

Carnelian

CRYSTAL **CLEANSING**

Cleansing crystals removes any energies they may have picked up on their journey to you. Use one of the following methods:

• Cleanse with water. Soak your crystals in a bowl of spring water for twenty-four hours for deep cleansing or hold them under a running tap for a few minutes, setting the intention that any negative imprints on them will be washed away. Some crystals are water soluble and/or affected by water, so don't use this method on selenite, halite malachite, gypsum, pyrite, optical calcite, or turquoise.

• Use sunlight or moonlight. Place your crystals outside in the sunlight for a few hours, or under the moonlight for a few hours or overnight. Some crystals are photosensitive, so don't use sunlight for amethyst, fluorite, rose quartz, or some calcites. And don't use sunlight for crystal balls, as this is a fire hazard.

• Try incense or smudging. Waft the smoke from a smudge stick or incense stick over your crystals, extinguishing it after use.

• Play singing bowls or ring bells. Place your crystals in a singing bowl and ring the outer or inner edge with the bowl's mallet to build up the sound, gradually increasing the speed. Or ring a bell in the same room as your crystals; the sound waves will shift any stagnation in the crystals.

• Use your breath. It's a go-to cleansing method when the above aren't practical: simply set your intention for the crystal and gently breathe on its surfaces.

• Do a white-light visualization. Visualize the crystal being purified by white light that comes first through you, then into the crystal. See any old, negative energy leave the crystal and disappear. You can combine this visualization with the breath method.

• Use a crystal cleanser spray. Use one that's specially formulated to cleanse crystals.

ATTUNING TO YOUR CRYSTALS

Hold each crystal in turn. Close your eyes and tune in to its vibration. You will find that you get a warmth and/or tingly feeling as you and your crystal connect energetically. Some people find that their crystal feels freezing cold. If you do not sense a physical change, which indicates a connection with the crystal, or an inner knowing that you are bonding, it's likely that the crystal is not right for you; set it aside. It may need further cleansing, or it may be best passed on to someone with whom it connects.

SETTING **YOUR INTENTION**

After cleansing and attuning your crystal, the next step is to set your intention. Hold each crystal in turn and say, "I work with this crystal for my highest good and that of others." This intention-setting programs your crystals for the positive work ahead.

CASTING THE STONES: TECHNIQUES

Here's how to cast the stones for a reading, whether you are reading for yourself or for another person:

- Choose a selection of crystals, place them in a small bowl, and tip them onto your mat. If you are reading for another person, ask her to choose the stones from your collection, place them in the bowl, and tip it onto the mat as she focuses on what she would like to know.

- Rather than use a bowl, shake—or have the questioner shake—the crystals with both hands and release them onto the mat, asking a question or for insight into a situation.

- For a past, present, future reading (see page 20), which doesn't interpret how the crystals fall, place your crystals in a purse or bag. Put your hand in the bag and, without looking, withdraw three or one at a time.

A SIMPLE YES-NO READING: THREE CRYSTALS

If you have a question that needs a straight answer, choose a black stone, a white stone, and another stone from your collection. Designate the black and white stones as yes and no; the black stone could mean yes and the white stone no or vice versa. The other stone you choose will be the deciding stone—its position in relation to the yes and no stones gives you your answer.

Palm the three stones and then cup both hands together and shake them, thinking of your question.

When you are ready, release the stones onto the mat. Where is the deciding stone? If it is closer to your yes stone, the answer to your question is yes. If it's closer to the no stone, the answer is no. If it is equidistant between yes and no, start again, casting the stones a maximum of three times. If after three tries you cannot obtain an answer, stop and try again another day; the answer is not yet known.

COUNTING THE RIPPLES: LECANOMANCY

Lecanomancy, meaning "dish" and "divination," is a form of hydromancy (see page 213). A meaning is assigned to the number of ripples around a stone dropped in water. Ask a yes-or-no question, gently drop one small crystal into a bowl of water, and immediately count the ripples. An odd number of ripples is a yes, and an even number means no.

This reading helps you see the most important issues and decisions around you now. It's not a straight predictive reading; its purpose is to help you see what needs to be done and how best to proceed. You can use nine or ten stones from your collection. Nine is the number of spirituality and intuition. As the last single-digit number before ten, it is also known as the number of culmination—the buildup before a resolution. Some crystal readers choose ten crystals, as ten represents wholeness; ten crystals tell a whole story. Alternatively, you can choose another number that intuitively feels right.

When you are ready, hold your question or inquiry in your mind. You might ask:

• What should I be focusing on now?

• How do I deal with (this) situation?

• What do I need to know?

Place your crystals into a small bowl or shake them in your cupped hands. Release them onto the mat. Interpret where they fall:

• The crystals closest to you, at the front of the mat, show what is at the forefront of your mind: the key issues that need addressing.

• Crystals in the center represent advice from the stones on how to address these concerns.

• Those farthest away from you show what is hidden or distant and may come into play in the future.

• Crystals that land off the mat are disregarded.

• Crystals that are partly on or off the mat are read as events that are coming your way but are not important yet.

Look up the interpretations of each crystal and/or hold each one in turn and see what you pick up intuitively. You might sense a crystal's meaning or its healing potential; you may sense colors or connect with particular memories. Crystals can be conduits to deep insights and past-life experiences. Be open to how your crystals communicate with you. Note your impressions.

You will also see that your crystals have formed little groups. Interpret them by what they have in common. For example, moonstone and lapis lazuli traditionally suggest a strong focus on spirituality, intuition, and dreams, so the pair shows the need to be guided by what is otherworldly or subconscious; there might be a message in a dream or a need to listen carefully to intuitive guidance. If peridot and selenite fall close together, you might take it that peridot means "disappointment" rather than "talent" because selenite tells us that we need to make changes to create more stability. The two stones together might tell a story of expectations not being met—and a need to make changes and move on. If these stones were at the front of the mat, this is a key issue that needs attention now. As with single stones, you might like to hold groups of crystals and feel if there is a strong, common message or sensation that links them.

CRYSTAL INSIGHTS: A QUICK READING

Cast your nine or ten stones onto the mat, but only interpret the three that fall closest to you (take the others off the mat).

Amethyst

What is hidden
or distant

Obsidian

Disregard
stones that fall
off the mat

Lapis Lazuli

Moonstone

Crystal advice

Hematite

Green Agate

Most
important
issues

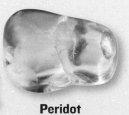

Peridot

Selentine

PAST, PRESENT, **FUTURE**

This simple reading helps you frame an event in the past, see what is happening in the present, and look at future influences.

Put all your crystals in a bag or purse and draw three, one at a time. Place the first stone on the left, the second stone in the center, and the third stone on the right, in a row.

Interpret all three crystals together, but this time, you have the advantage of a timeline. For example, you might have bloodstone, smoky quartz, and citrine (as shown). Bloodstone means resilience, smoky quartz means patience and resources, and citrine means money and manifesting. In response to the question, "Can my new business idea grow?" one interpretation would be:

"Your business has been hard work (the past); now, you may need to see results, but you need to be patient—you have the resources to hold your position (the present); the successful business you want will come. Keep manifesting this through dedication and have confidence (future)."

This is based on the traditional meanings of the stones, but you may also use meanings that intuitively arise at the time of your reading. Go with what feels right.

Past
1
Bloodstone

Present
2
Smoky Quartz

Future
3
Citrine

CRYSTAL **ADVICE**

This three-stone reading also uses three positions, but it assigns different meanings to each crystal.

Draw three crystals, one at a time. Ask about "me/my situation" before drawing the first stone. Ask about external influences before drawing the second (frame this as you like: "what other people think" or "how friends are influencing me," for example). The third crystal is advice from outside yourself and others: a message that the crystal itself brings you. See the interpretations for the crystals on page 28 or work with your intuitive responses.

Me/my situation	External influences	Crystal advice
1	**2**	**3**

WHAT'S HELPING YOU AND WHAT'S NOT

This developed past, present, future reading reveals what is helping and hindering your progress. It's helpful to see this reading in terms of attitudes and beliefs, rather than to try to fit specific events to the stones' meanings. Be open to what might arise during your interpretations.

You can lay out the crystals one of two ways. Either select five crystals from your bag or purse and place them in the order shown below on your mat or shake the five crystals in your hands and drop them one at a time, placing them in the following positions:

North
Future
5

West
Obstacles
3

Center
The present
1

East
What is helping you
4

South
Past influences
2

THE ASTROLOGICAL READING: THE HOUSES OF THE SELF

For this reading, cast your stones over the astrological wheel and interpret them according to the zodiac sign, or house, in which they fall. By combining the stone and the astrological house, you get to see how the stone's meaning relates to an area of life.

Choose twelve stones from your purse or bag and then shake them, asking, for example, "What do I need to know now?" and cast them over the diagram below.

Ignore any crystals that fall outside the wheel and interpret those that clearly fall within the marked sectors. For example, if you have amethyst in the Sixth house, you may interpret this as a need to address stress to improve your health; it's also known as the healer's stone, calling you to heal yourself. For those who are healing practitioners, amethyst may ask you to work on your self-healing for a while.

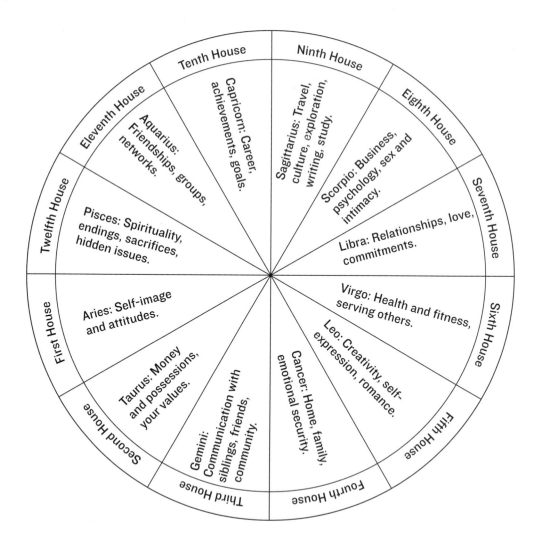

THE BA GUA: REALIZING YOUR FULL POTENTIAL

The Ba Gua, a map of life used in Feng Shui, offers a way to look at life areas including love, money, and fame. You can do a simple crystal reading to see which areas will be most auspicious for you. The crystal guides you toward your highest potential in the area in which it falls, as if saying, "if you adopt this approach, you can achieve success in this area."

Choose eight crystals and cast them onto the Ba Gua below or copy it and place it over your reading mat. Ignore any crystals that fall outside the map and interpret those that clearly fall within the marked sectors. For example, if you had carnelian in the career square, the message could be to take a risk to get to the next level. Citrine on the love square gives you a "yes" if you're wondering if a relationship will happen, and it predicts optimism and happiness in partnerships.

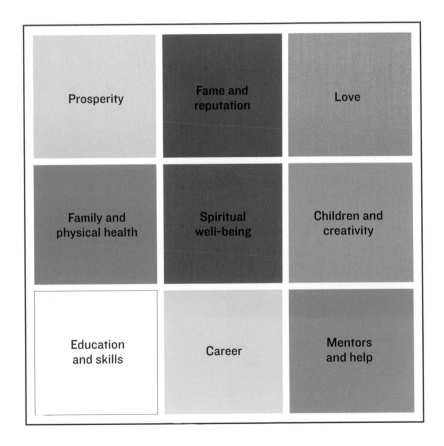

A MEDICINE WHEEL READING

This layout is based upon the Medicine Wheel, which divides into four realms—physical, emotional, intellectual, and spiritual. It's a great reading to do when you're feeling vaguely unsettled, without a specific question, as it helps you see how you are affected and what might be the cause.

Choose four stones from your bag or purse, one at a time. Shake them all in your cupped hands and drop them over the illustration (or copy it and place it over your mat). Look at the sectors on which the crystals appear (you can disregard any that fall outside the wheel). The crystal suggests what you need— a stone in the body sector would advise you what your body needs, while a crystal in the emotions sector would suggest what you need for emotional stability and happiness. Then, interpret the crystal according to each section. Look up the stone meanings on page 28 and interpret them. For example, if you got tiger's eye as one of your mind sector stones, one interpretation would be you need to go deep to discover the true motivation behind a person's behavior or to ask what's beneath your surface; do you need to be more resilient?

When you have interpreted your crystals, take them from the mat and hold them together. Tune in to their energy and note any further impressions you are given. Let your intuition guide you toward any positive action that may support your healing needs.

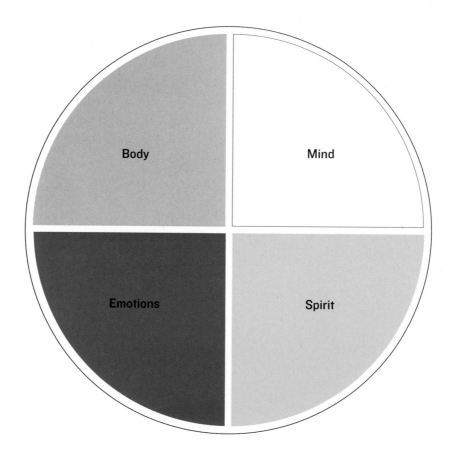

A CHAKRA CRYSTAL READING

An easy way to interpret your crystals is purely by their colors, which can be linked with the seven major chakras, or energy points, in the body. First, take out all your crystals with these dominant colors.

Next, formulate your question, for example, "What life area do I need to focus on now?" or "Where's my block?" Finally, choose three stones out of the bag and cast them (see page 15). Which colors of crystal dominate? Use the chart below to interpret the colors in light of your question.

Chakra Color	Example	Meaning
Red	Garnet	Security, belonging, money, home
Orange	Carnelian, orange calcite	Identity, nurturing, fertility, ideas
Yellow	Citrine	Physical strength, energy, willpower
Green and/or pink	Rose quartz, emerald	Love and relationships
Blue	Sodalite, blue lace agate	Communication, speaking your truth
Purple	Amethyst, purple fluorite	Intuition, inner wisdom
White or clear	Clear quartz, moonstone	Spirituality, guidance, oneness

FOUR-ELEMENT DIVINATION

Here's another approach: Group your crystals according to their color and then to each of the four elements—Earth, Fire, Air, and Water. Do this intuitively, according to how each crystal feels. For example, Fire stones might be all your reds and oranges, Earth stones all the greens, Water stones all the blues and whites, and Air stones all the yellows. Black stones are often associated with grounding and protection, so you might assign these to the Earth element. Cast your stones (see page 15) and interpret them according to your personal association with the elements or by these suggestions:

Earth: The physical and material realm. Practical concerns, the home and possessions, staying grounded.

Fire: The realm of the soul. Desire, passion, drive, enterprise.

Air: The realm of the mind. Thought, strategy, intelligence, research.

Water: The realm of the heart. Love, emotions, sensitivity, and the relationship with the self and others.

You can pendulum-dowse (see page 41) over a group of crystals to divine which stone or stones has a message for you. First, choose twelve crystals from your collection. Include citrine, if you have it (as this means yes in response to a question in a reading), or designate another stone as your yes crystal; then, choose a black or white crystal to represent no. When you are dowsing, you are then free to ask a closed yes-no question or a broader question, for example, "What do I need to focus on now?" or "Are there any hidden issues I need to know about?"

Place your yes and no crystals opposite one another. Choose the other ten crystals at random and place them in a circle, like a clock face, with your yes and no crystals 180 degrees apart.

Hold the pendulum in the center above the circle and ask your question. Allow the pendulum to move freely and note if it swings toward one or more crystals. If you're unsure, you can remove a crystal from the circle and ask it if you should

interpret it—dowse over it and use your yes or no position (see page 17).

Take a note of the crystal the pendulum swings toward in response to your question. For example, if you got lepidolite, the message would be to heal or lower stress (and this may well come up first in a reading, as stress often blocks our ability to deal with other issues or make progress toward goals).

Your pendulum may swing toward more than one crystal, but to keep things simple, go with a maximum of three crystals your pendulum identifies. These represent the strongest responses to your question. For example, if you asked, "What do I need to focus on now?" three crystals are enough; otherwise, you may become unfocused with too many possibilities. After your reading, you may hold your chosen stone or stones and see what further impressions or messages arise for you.

Purple Fluorite

Amber

Carnelian

Rose Quartz

Jade

**Black Tourmaline
"NO"**

**Citrine
"YES"**

Green Agate

Amethyst

Lapis Lazuli

Moonstone

Turquoise

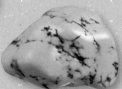

CRYSTAL MEANINGS IN DIVINATION

Here are suggested meanings for crystals used in divination. There are varying associations between crystals and zodiac signs, based on ruling planets, birthstones, and other traditional sources, so the astrological associations listed here are for guidance and are not intended to be definitive. The interpretations are intended, also, to act as a starting point for an intuitive connection with the stones: As you work with them, you may devise your own personal meanings for your crystal readings.

AGATE (VARIOUS COLORS)

Zodiac signs: Gemini, Capricorn

Divinatory meaning: Success, prosperity

Agate is associated with success and abundance, reaching goals, and being well rewarded. It also shows a connection with the earth and the environment, so it reveals a grounded, can-do attitude. You may also find that being in nature helps you replenish and grow emotionally and spiritually.

AGATE, BLUE LACE (BLUE)

Zodiac signs: Gemini, Pisces

Divinatory meaning: News, communication

Communications and news arrive via emails, letters, and messages or direct conversation. You may need to express your feelings and ideas sensitively; work out what you need to say to negotiate a delicate situation and avoid misunderstandings. There is support around you.

AGATE, FIRE (RED, ORANGE, GREEN, BLUE)

Zodiac signs: Aries, Leo

Divinatory meaning: Secret fears

It is time to express and release buried doubts or fears. Communicating your concerns comes with a risk of rejection, but speaking your truth empowers you. Your words clear away confusion and create an opportunity for future security. Call upon your inner strength to voice your fears.

AGATE, MOSS (GREEN)

Zodiac sign: Virgo

Divinatory meaning: Finding treasure

Your treasure may be talents or inner resources or a desired goal. As this crystal is traditionally known as the gardener's stone, you may find literal treasure in the earth or discover a relationship with the natural world that inspires your imagination. Trees and rituals that honor the seasons connect you with your Self.

AMAZONITE (GREEN, BLUE)

Zodiac sign: Virgo

Divinatory meaning: Trust in the universe

Adventures beckon, but worry and anxiety may be blocking your progress. This is unnecessary, as this stone predicts good outcomes in examinations or other tests. Trust yourself. You may be called to divination, clairvoyance, or other creative and compassionate pursuits that rely on clear communication. The work you dream of awaits.

AMBER (YELLOW, ORANGE-YELLOW)

Zodiac signs: Taurus, Leo, Aquarius

Divinatory meaning: Protection, potential

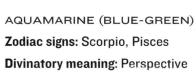

Your innate wisdom can say who and what are best for you. You may be considering positive changes to your lifestyle and assessing certain relationships just now; protect yourself from any negativity or friendships that drain you. Amber is also a stone of potential—there's a light within you that is ready to shine.

AMETHYST (PURPLE)

Zodiac signs: Aries, Sagittarius, Pisces, Aquarius

Divinatory meaning: Spirituality

Amethyst is a stone of intuition that acknowledges spiritual awareness. You may be involved in compassionate work, such as healing, or be ready to develop your intuitive abilities; a creative project may help you deepen your spiritual connection. The stone can also indicate stress and the need to recharge physically and emotionally.

APATITE (BLUE)

Zodiac sign: Gemini

Divinatory meaning: Inner truth

Apatite says that the truth is within you. This quiet stone offers you an opportunity to incubate a problem or an idea and, if needed, heal from within. Give yourself time to come to your own conclusions rather than assume other people have the answers. Commit to yourself and speak your truth when you are ready.

AQUAMARINE (BLUE-GREEN)

Zodiac signs: Scorpio, Pisces

Divinatory meaning: Perspective

Take a step back and look again. A situation may not be perfect, but with a new perspective, you may see that it is good enough. In relationships, aquamarine is associated with reconnection, so a love bond is repaired or deepened. The stone also suggests travel and protection on your journey, particularly over water.

AVENTURINE, GREEN

Zodiac signs: Aries, Virgo, Libra

Divinatory meaning: Luck, success

Aventurine brings wealth, harmony, and an opportunity to take the lead. With new responsibility comes calculated risks, but luck will be on your side and you'll enjoy success. The stone can also show a need for healing and rebalancing; know that peaceful times are coming. A stressful situation will soon be over.

BLOODSTONE (AKA HELIOTROPE; GREEN-RED)

Zodiac signs: Aries, Libra, Pisces

Divinatory meaning: Resilience

A crystal of courage, consistency, and resilience, bloodstone asks you to keep going. Draw upon your energy and wisdom, be relentless, and you can achieve your purpose. You may need to protect yourself from ill health by conserving your energy or to guard against unfair criticism you give or receive. Better communication is always possible.

CALCITE (VARIED COLORS)

Zodiac signs: Gemini, Cancer, Leo, Pisces

Divinatory meaning: Identity, creativity

Calcite is a memory stone; it asks you to remember who you are. You may have experienced a loss of identity through changing roles or lifestyle and need more space to follow your own pursuits. Calcite also suggests creative projects.

The varieties of calcite have the following meanings:

Blue: Messages from your guides

Orange: Try again; the need to do something twice

Pink: Love and forgiveness; vulnerability; time to let go of sadness

Yellow: Patience; protection

CARNELIAN, ORANGE/RED

Zodiac signs: Leo, Virgo, Capricorn

Divinatory meaning: Risk, self-belief

Take a risk and you will succeed. You intuitively know what to do; just listen to your inner guidance. If you feel stressed and blocked, muster your self-confidence and take that leap of faith. Carnelian's positivity also embraces legal decisions, negotiations, agreements, and any decision that means giving yourself more of what you need to live life in balance.

CELESTITE, BLUE/WHITE

Zodiac signs: Gemini, Aquarius

Divinatory meaning: Angelic messages

Celestite is the stone of heaven, and it can reveal a spiritual connection; you may receive messages from angels and spirits and feel angels' unconditional love and guidance through synchronicities and unexpected help from those around you.

This crystal also suggests imagination, dream recall, and messages through dreams.

CHALCEDONY, BLUE

Zodiac signs: Gemini, Cancer, Sagittarius

Divinatory meaning: Reconnection

Chalcedony brings reunions, and you reconnect with a significant person from the past. In general, the stone shows you have a need to talk  and fully express yourself; you may need to communicate gently rather than be forthright. Additional meanings include new information and learning through education.

CHRYSOCOLLA (GREEN, BLUE, TURQUOISE)

Zodiac signs: Taurus, Gemini, Virgo

Divinatory meaning: A reality check

Chrysocolla can tell you that you are doing too much. It's now time to stop and prioritize your projects and responsibilities rather than  continue to give. Are you unknowingly sabotaging yourself? You have an opportunity to put yourself first by setting boundaries and saying no, gently but firmly.

CHRYSOPRASE (GREEN)

Zodiac signs: Gemini, Cancer, Aquarius

Divinatory meaning: Optimism, partnership

Chrysoprase is believed to hold goddess energy, bestowing love, self-acceptance, and self-worth. It signifies cheerfulness,  abundance, good health, and happy partnerships, so your relationships thrive. The stone also foretells clear purpose, the beginning of imaginative projects, and a good decision made.

CITRINE (YELLOW, YELLOW-BROWN)

Zodiac signs: Aries, Gemini, Leo, Virgo

Divinatory meaning: Manifesting, money

This stone of prosperity and communication gives you a "yes" to any question you might ask in a reading. It also predicts money,  sales, and material comforts, which in turn lift your confidence and mood. Citrine also tells you that now is the right time to manifest, with good intentions, whatever you want.

EMERALD (GREEN)

Zodiac signs: Taurus, Gemini, Aries, Cancer

Divinatory meaning: Promises

Emerald reveals commitment, so a confidence or promise is kept. In relationships, you speak the truth and honor your own truth. The stone is also linked with finding and retaining information, so you may be researching or studying a subject close to your heart. Additional meanings include success, happiness, and fertility.

FLUORITE, GREEN

Zodiac sign: Pisces

Divinatory meaning: Renewal

Green fluorite says you are renewing and even reinventing yourself after a period of contemplation or solitude; you emerge stronger and wiser. A new relationship or creative opportunity arrives, but take your time before responding. Be sure that this offer is worthy of you.

FLUORITE, PURPLE

Zodiac sign: Pisces

Divinatory meaning: Expansion, purpose

Stay focused on your goals and wishes, as you are on the brink of a breakthrough. It is now time to expand your horizons and realize what you are

capable of—intellectually and spiritually. You may have a skill you could make money from or use to help others. Know and honor your life purpose.

GARNET, RED

Zodiac signs: Aries, Leo, Sagittarius, Capricorn, Aquarius

Divinatory meaning: Emotional balance

Love, passion, anger—powerful emotions abound. You may need to make a personal sacrifice to regain your balance or make peace. Commitment is important to you now. Garnet can also show either a new romance or in existing partnerships, a temporary separation due to circumstance rather than choice.

HEMATITE (DARK SILVER, RED)

Zodiac sign: Capricorn, Aries

Divinatory meaning: Grounding

Stay grounded, regardless of all the calls upon your attention. Your past knowledge and experience support you, but being rooted in the here-and-now brings new opportunities into focus—and you have the drive and willpower to make the most of them. The stone is also linked with the earth and appreciating the gifts of nature.

JADE, GREEN (AKA NEPHRITE, JADEITE)

Zodiac signs: Aries, Taurus, Libra

Divinatory meaning: Love

Jade is a stone of love, romance, and compassion. Relationships are central to your life just now, and you take a heart-centered approach beyond personal partnerships, showing kindness to those who do not love themselves enough. Additional meanings include luck and well-being.

JASPER, RED

Zodiac sign: Aries, Scorpio

Divinatory meaning: Intensity

You may need to deal with intense emotions such as anger, guilt, or jealousy; these emotions may be yours or expressed by someone close to you. Step back from the maelstrom and you will see what to do and what not to do. With new insight, a situation or relationship can be restored or rescued.

JASPER, YELLOW

Zodiac sign: Leo, Sagittarius

Divinatory meaning: Blocks

Yellow jasper can reveal blocks to your progress: an energetic block that has a physical impact, such as low energy, low mood, and poor motivation; a creative block, when projects and ideas feel stuck; or feeling, generally, disconnected from spiritual or inner guidance. You may

need to release yourself from pressure to perform or to be a certain way to get back in the flow. Yellow jasper can also mean a travel opportunity.

JET (BLACK)

Zodiac sign: Capricorn

Divinatory meaning: Endings

Jet says you may be holding on to powerful or negative feelings that need to be released. A situation has ended, and you search for stability during this transition period; this will come as you allow the emotions to arise and when you are ready, let them go. Jet is also linked with psychic protection and psychic connection.

KUNZITE, PINK

Zodiac signs: Aries, Taurus, Leo, Libra, Scorpio

Divinatory meaning: Peace

Peace is coming: Trust in the universe, surrender, and see where things lead. This stone says you are attracting love at a higher level, calling in a soul mate, and generating more self-love, unconditional love, and compassion for others. If you have been suffering from stress, serenity will return.

LABRADORITE (AKA SPECTROLITE; BLACK, BLUE, YELLOW IRIDESCENT)

Zodiac signs: Sagittarius, Capricorn, Aquarius, Pisces

Divinatory meaning: Change

Your expectations are shifting. Someone is not as they seem, so be discerning, as what you are told may be exaggerated or false. Protect yourself from other people's negative energies. The stone can also show news and creative skills that bring success. Expect great changes.

LAPIS LAZULI (BLUE, GOLD)

Zodiac signs: Taurus, Libra, Sagittarius, Aquarius

Divinatory meaning: Insights

Lapis, the heavenly stone, brings insights in dreams and reaffirms your spiritual connection.

You may be recalling someone from the past and questioning your relationship with them, seeing this person in a new light; if so, it is time to express your thoughts. A stone of truth, lapis lazuli supports the intellect and guides you to stand up for what you believe in.

LEPIDOLITE (PINK, PURPLE)

Zodiac sign: Libra

Divinatory meaning: Healing

This stone can show stress, anxiety, and the need for healing. There may be a need to break negative thought patterns and position yourself so you do not become embroiled in old dramas.

You find a place of calm within. You may also discover or further develop your spiritual connection.

MALACHITE (GREEN)

Zodiac signs: Scorpio, Sagittarius, Capricorn

Divinatory meaning: Challenges, creativity

Trouble is averted; you manage a challenging person or situation and discover not only who your friends are, but your knack for an inventive solution. Partnerships and creative projects thrive, and you may sense a deep, subconscious guidance. Malachite can also mean money.

MOONSTONE (WHITE, YELLOW, CREAM, BLUE, GREEN)

Zodiac signs: Cancer, Virgo, Libra, Scorpio, Aquarius, Pisces

Divinatory meaning: Harmony, friendship

Moonstone brings harmony, new friends, openness, and flexibility. It is linked with sensitivity, intuition, and dreams, and it can show issues beneath the surface that you are ready to deal with; an old situation may be transformed. A new idea or plan may also be emerging.

34

OBSIDIAN, APACHE TEAR (BLACK)

Zodiac sign: Scorpio

Divinatory meaning: Grief

Apache tear denotes dealing with grief, frustration, and fear. You may feel you have little or no control over events and feel vulnerable and highly sensitive. The message, however, is that you are protected and can recover a sense of security. The stone is also associated with psychic protection.

OBSIDIAN, BLACK

Zodiac signs: Scorpio, Capricorn

Divinatory meaning: Hidden influences, revelations

Obsidian shows you may be acknowledging strong emotions or hidden influences that, if released, can bring positive change. Clearing these past issues may need a slow, gentle approach. Additional meanings include sacred contracts, karmic lessons, cutting attachment ties, and divination.

ONYX (BLACK, GRAY, BLUE, WHITE, YELLOW, BROWN, RED)

Zodiac signs: Leo, Capricorn

Divinatory meaning: Inner wisdom

There may be something you've had to learn or are in the process of learning the hard way, which

has brought confusion and even panic. Onyx says you are in a stronger position than you think. Turn inward and connect with your personal power; be self-contained and follow your inner guidance.

OPAL, BLUE

Zodiac signs: Virgo, Libra

Divinatory meaning: A wish come true

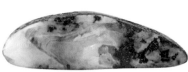

Opal magnifies ideas and increases emotions, ideas, and sensitivity, reassuring you that you can manifest your wishes. You may experience a creative surge and enter a dreamy, imaginative phase that offers new insights. This stone is also connected with clairvoyant ability and can also signify loyalty.

The following opal colors have these meanings:

Fire: Hopes

Pink: Wish for psychic connection

PERIDOT, GREEN (AKA CHRYSOLITE, OLIVINE)

Zodiac signs: Virgo, Libra, Capricorn, Taurus

Divinatory meaning: Self-reliance

Disappointment leads to a recognition of your worth. A relationship may not be what you had hoped, but you fortify yourself from within; you may assert your identity and creativity doing work that you love. A particular skill or talent brings you deserved rewards.

QUARTZ, CLEAR

Zodiac signs: Cancer, Aquarius, Pisces

Divinatory meaning: Powerful clarity

Clear quartz brings the ability to manifest what you want and build upon what you have, following and knowing your true purpose. A new journey begins and major changes await. You are protected while you follow your path, and you are blessed with clarity; you will see exactly where you need to go.

QUARTZ, ROSE (PINK)

Zodiac signs: Taurus, Virgo

Divinatory meaning: Love, reconciliation

The love crystal, rose quartz, brings you a new relationship and an opportunity to heal the old wounds of your heart. Self-love and self-esteem flourish, and you share love unconditionally with others. You receive loving support in your endeavors. An additional meaning is forgiveness.

QUARTZ, RUTILATED (AKA ANGEL HAIR; GOLDEN/DARK STRANDS)

Zodiac signs: Gemini, Virgo

Divinatory meaning: Inspiration

You are inspired to take an idea a step further or leap into a new creative venture. Your insights multiply and you feel connected spiritually, while making new connections with people as your network expands. Rutilated quartz also sees you analyzing a situation from all angles.

QUARTZ, SMOKY (YELLOW, BROWN)

Zodiac signs: Libra, Sagittarius, Capricorn

Divinatory meaning: Patience

Smoky quartz predicts a quiet phase when things move slowly. The changes you want to see will happen, but gradually, when the timing is right. You may feel a need to retreat to conserve your energy, to withdraw so you can recharge. Be patient and all will become clear.

RHODOCHROSITE (PINK, ORANGE)

Zodiac signs: Cancer, Leo, Scorpio

Divinatory meaning: Forgiveness and love

Rhodochrosite shows you can heal old wounds and have the relationships you deserve. You may need to forgive yourself, but do not feel you must take responsibility for everything; believe that you deserve the good things. Appreciate, too, the love and comfort around you.

RHODONITE (PINK, RED)

Zodiac signs: Taurus, Cancer

Divinatory meaning: Sharing

Rhodonite brings the gift of love and sees you finding your true passion in life. This may be expressed within a relationship or in acts of service, from showing compassion for others to teaching or healing. You are now in a position not only to attract love, but to discover your deepest motivations.

SELENITE, WHITE

Zodiac signs: Cancer, Taurus

Divinatory meaning: Fixing instability

This stone of spiritual connection says you may have to make changes to create more security for yourself. This may mean you see what or who is supportive now and what must stay in the past;

you will gently be able to let go of what you no longer need. New horizons beckon.

SODALITE (BLUE)

Zodiac signs: Virgo, Sagittarius

Divinatory meaning: The right words

Sodalite is a stone of communication, so it is time to express your ideas. You may need to find a way to translate a concept into plain language, or in relationships, speak the truth as you see it. The stone can show problems being solved and a determination to break new ground.

SUNSTONE (YELLOW, ORANGE, BROWNISH)

Zodiac signs: Libra, Pisces

Divinatory meaning: Being of service

Sunstone shows you are manifesting wealth and abundance; conscious of your worth, you know the contribution you can make. You are warm toward others who need your help, so you may be of service, sharing your wisdom and offering leadership. If you have been through a testing time, sunstone reassures you that all will be well.

TIGER'S EYE, BROWN-GOLD

Zodiac signs: Gemini, Taurus, Leo

Divinatory meaning: Evidence

The stone of energy, protection, and confidence, tiger's eye asks you to go beyond appearances to discover the true nature of an issue; look for the evidence  beneath the surface glimmer. You call upon your inner strength to see what is hidden and make a decision that protects your interests. Additional meanings include prosperity and happiness.

The following varieties of tiger's eye have these meanings:

Blue: Relief from anxiety

Red: Motivation; feeling overwhelmed; need for balance

TOURMALINE, BLACK

Zodiac sign: Capricorn

Divinatory meaning: Focus, protection

Protect yourself from negativity and be aware of any negative thought patterns. Attend to what is important to you. Be resilient and stay grounded and in the present.
You don't need to close down to protect yourself, however. You can stay open to the good things in life within safe boundaries. It could also mean a situation coming to an end.

Other varieties of tourmaline have these meanings:

Green: Growth; results

Pink: Compassion; love; beginnings

TURQUOISE

Zodiac signs: Taurus, Leo, Scorpio, Sagittarius, Capricorn, Pisces

Divinatory meaning: Prosperity, protection

Turquoise is traditionally a stone of prosperity and protection. In divination, it asks you to guard your possessions and deflect negativity. You may need to tackle tasks you have been avoiding  to clear the way for the success that awaits you. Turquoise can also show productivity and creative skill, and it predicts journeys.

UNAKITE (GREEN-PINK)

Zodiac sign: Scorpio

Divinatory meaning: Compromise

Unakite can reveal stress, anxiety, and feeling unsupported. You may want to break free of a pattern, or you may need to change the way you work. However, rather than go to extremes to win back your freedom, begin with a compromise. Small adjustments can have a big impact.

CRYSTAL **DIRECTORY**

Use a pendulum over this directory to find a stone that calls to you or to get a divinatory message.

GREEN AGATE	BLUE LACE AGATE	FIRE AGATE
MOSS AGATE	AMAZONITE	AMBER
AMETHYST	BLUE APATITE	AQUAMARINE
AVENTURINE	BLOODSTONE	YELLOW CALCITE
CARNELIAN	CELESTITE	BLUE CHALCEDONY
CHRYSOCOLLA	CHRYSOPRASE	CITRINE
EMERALD	GREEN FLUORITE	PURPLE FLUORITE
GARNET	HEMATITE	JADE
RED JASPER	YELLOW JASPER	JET
PINK KUNZITE	LABRADORITE	LAPIS LAZULI
LEPIDOLITE	MALACHITE	MOONSTONE
APACHE TEAR OBSIDIAN	BLACK OBSIDIAN	ONYX
BLUE OPAL	PERIDOT	CLEAR QUARTZ
ROSE QUARTZ	RUTILATED QUARTZ	SMOKY QUARTZ
RHODOCHROSITE	RHODONITE	SELENITE
SODALITE	SUNSTONE	TIGER'S EYE
BLACK TOURMALINE	TURQUOISE	UNAKITE

DIVINATION WITH A PENDULUM

Pendulum divination is a form of dowsing, or "finding." We dowse with a pendulum to find an answer to a question. Anyone can learn to use a pendulum. When you hold one, you can become a channel for higher wisdom; energy flows through your body, down your arm and hand, and into the pendulum. The quality of this energy causes the pendulum to move in formations or directions that you can interpret, usually as a simple yes or no response.

CHOOSING A PENDULUM

You can use virtually any small object as a pendulum, provided it has enough weight and can be attached to a chain, cord, string, ribbon, or thread. Try a ring on a chain or delve into your jewelry box for a pendant necklace. If your improvised pendulum feels right, dedicate it as a pendulum for the time you need it (simply ask it to work with you for your higher good) and begin.

Most ready-made pendulums are shaped like a downward cone. They may be smooth or faceted, and some come with engraved or painted symbols. Common materials are crystal and metals such as brass, silver, or copper, and some practitioners prefer wood. You might prefer a pendulum with an additional small round ball or stone at the other end; it sits between your index and middle fingers, giving you a relaxed finger position as you dowse.

You can choose your crystal pendulum according to the crystal's qualities. Amethyst and clear quartz are popular choices, because they relate to the third eye and crown chakra points, which are linked with intuition and spiritual connection. Alternatively, select a pendulum that aligns with your question. For example, rose quartz is associated with the heart, so you might use it for relationship questions.

HOW TO DOWSE WITH A PENDULUM

Cleanse the pendulum. Gently wipe it so it is clean and dust-free. Visualize white light sweeping through it and taking away any negative or old vibrations.

1 Attune the pendulum. Hold it with your thumb and index finger, or any way that is comfortable; you might prefer to wind the top of the chain around your index finger to secure it, for example. Rest your elbow on a table so your arm is supported and the pendulum is free to move. Take a breath and sense that you are opening up to the pendulum's energy, allowing your higher consciousness to direct its movement. Ask a question with a known yes response; for example, "Is my name Melissa/Sean/Alicia?" See how it moves; this is its yes response. Repeat with a no question. (If you get the same movement for yes and no, the pendulum you're using isn't right for you.) Give the pendulum up to thirty seconds to settle into its swing response. It may do one of the following things:

• Swing diagonally.

• Make a counterclockwise circle.

• Make a clockwise circle.

2 Ask your question. Take a breath. Try to let go of any expectations you may have about the answer you'd like to your question. Carefully consider your question before you dowse with the pendulum. You might simplify it by breaking it down. For example, if you were thinking about career opportunities—should you try to get a promotion, look for alternative work, or go self-employed—you might ask, "Do I need to make a major decision about work?" When you have your answer, you can formulate your next simple question, such as, "Should I consider a new job?"

WHAT IF **THE ANSWER IS NOT CLEAR?**

If the pendulum doesn't move in an obvious direction, ask your question again, up to three times, until you see a yes or no. If your pendulum barely moves or gives a slight tremble, now is not the time for this question.

INFLUENCING THE PENDULUM

You can influence a pendulum when you're attached to an outcome. Say you ask a question and you don't like the answer; you ask again, and this time it gives the answer you want, but this second answer proves incorrect. You've subconsciously directed the outcome.

If you think you have too much emotionally invested in an answer, ask a friend to dowse for you. This works exceptionally well because you do not voice your question; your friend's pendulum responds just to your question, rather than your need. Your friend can use her own pendulum or attune to yours (see page 41). Stand or sit close to her and do not tell her your question. In your mind, silently ask the question, looking at your friend as she holds the pendulum, and see what it says.

FINDING LOST OBJECTS WITH A PENDULUM

Try to let go of any anxiety you're feeling about the lost item. Take a moment to sit, be calm, empty your mind, and take a few deep breaths. To begin, hold your pendulum and, naming your item, ask:

"Is it possible for [the item] to be found?"

"Is it in this house/office?"

If yes, move to one area, asking:

"Is [my item] in this room?"

If no, walk to another room and ask again. Stand still as you wait for the pendulum to answer. Then narrow down your search criteria —for example, asking if it's in the corner of the room. Then go to that corner and ask the pendulum to direct you to the object.

PENDULUM **DOWSING WITH AFFIRMATION CARDS**

If you have a set of angel cards, you can use your pendulum to pinpoint a guiding message. Shuffle your cards and spread them out on a table, facedown. Hold your pendulum above them and ask which message or angel you need. Allow the pendulum to move and see which card or cards it moves toward. If the pendulum moves toward a group of cards, take this group, placing the other cards aside, and separate the cards. Repeat the question and see which card the pendulum directs you toward. To check you have selected the right card, ask the pendulum if this card is right for you and see if it gives you your yes response.

GOING **BEYOND YES OR NO ANSWERS**

Pendulum charts offer a way to get beyond the closed question and select from a host of possibilities. There are many pendulum charts online, showing, for example, degrees of yes or no, relationship compatibility, flower remedies, crystals, or essential oils. The chart below corresponds to the seven principal chakra points, or energy centers, of the body and their associated life areas. You can use it or compile your own chart or grid, personalizing the answers to suit you.

To use the chart, hold your pendulum at the bottom of the semicircle. Ask your question and see if the pendulum swings toward one of the chart segments. If so, hold your pendulum over that segment and ask for confirmation that this is your answer.

Questions you might ask:

• What do I need most in my life now?

• Is there anything blocking me?

• What should I focus on?

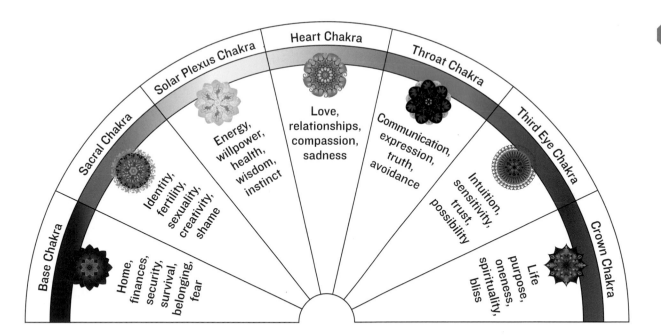

Heart Chakra
Love, relationships, compassion, sadness

Solar Plexus Chakra
Energy, willpower, health, wisdom, instinct

Throat Chakra
Communication, expression, truth, avoidance

Sacral Chakra
Identity, fertility, sexuality, creativity, shame

Third Eye Chakra
Intuition, sensitivity, trust, possibility

Base Chakra
Home, finances, security, survival, belonging, fear

Crown Chakra
Life, purpose, oneness, spirituality, bliss

MAKING YOUR OWN PENDULUM CHART

When you need guidance to choose between several courses of action, your pendulum can help. First, write down your options on a semi-circular template, shown here, which you can scan or photocopy. For example, a set of options might look like this:

• Make no changes at this time.

• Pursue a job application now.

• Look for a position in my present company.

• Go self-employed.

• Take advice.

• Consider a temporary position.

• Consider this later in the year.

You can include more options, but keeping it to around seven or eight means you'll clearly see which segment your pendulum swings toward. Take time to consider your options carefully before you write them on the chart, as this process can often help clarify your situation even before you ask your pendulum.

Hold the pendulum above the semicircle, aligned centrally at the base of the circle, ask your question, and then ask your pendulum to swing toward the option that is right for you. Hold the pendulum above that option and ask, "Is this the right choice now?" Note its response.

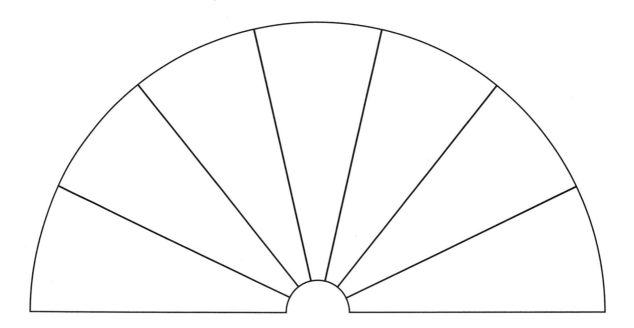

DIVINATION WITH RUNES

The runes, a sequence of literal and symbolic letters, are the ancient sacred alphabet of the Germanic peoples of northern Europe. They were used for divination and magic; the word *rune* derives from the Gothic word *runa*, meaning "secret" or "mystery."

In the Poetic Edda, a collection of Old Norse minstrel poems, runes are inscribed to make powerful talismans and amulets of protection. They're etched on a sword hilt to win a battle, written on the palms of a mother to deliver her baby safely, and burned on the oars of fishermen for safe journeys across the waves. Rune inscriptions survive on wood, bone, coins, weapons, rings, and hundreds of Viking-age memorial rune stones found predominantly in Scandinavia.

Mediterranean traders used runes for casting lots (divining for decisions), and they likely introduced them into Scandinavia, Iceland, western Europe, and northern England. Regardless of the Christianization of Europe and the adoption of the Latin alphabet, runes survived; the last rune masters and mistresses—those who divined with runes—endured until around three hundred years ago.

As Germanic languages developed, so did the runes; thus, we have variations in letter formation and the number of runes in a set, or Futhark. Futhark is an acronym after the first six letters of the runic alphabet: Fehu, Uruz, Thurisaz, Ansuz, Raido, and Kaunaz.

TYPES OF RUNE TO BUY OR MAKE

Futharks are commonly available in natural stone, lightweight fiberglass, wood, ceramic, and crystal; some diviners use cards with runic inscriptions, but many prefer the feel of natural materials and purchase them from independent craftspeople. Traditionally, the runic letters are painted red.

You can make your own runes by painting the letters on pebbles from the beach or on pieces of found wood from a fruit-bearing tree. The pieces don't have to be uniform or cut to a regular size, but they will need to be smaller than your palm for easy handling and laying out. Using a knife, carefully pare away some of the bark so you have a surface for your inscription. You can also use a pyrography tool, which burns wood like a pen, rather than paint your letters.

What of the blank rune, Wyrd? Although there is no historical evidence for the existence of a blank rune, and its meaning is covered by Pertho (see page 54), some rune sets include it to represent the unknown, or "wyrd." If you have a blank rune in your set, you can use it or ignore it. If you choose to use it, give some thought to how you might interpret it, given the overlap with Pertho. One approach is to assign it as "the answer to [my] question is unknown at this time" or simply as "silence," perhaps advice from the runes to stay silent on the matter in question.

A NOTE ON THE INTERPRETATIONS

Although runes are their own system, developing years before and independently from tarot cards, I include my personal tarot associations to help those of you familiar with tarot but not runes, as a point of reference.

THE ELDER FUTHARK

The Elder Futhark of twenty-four runes is arranged in three sets of eight, or aetts. They are named Frey, Hagalaz, and Tyr. Some of the rune meanings derive from key runic poems: the Norwegian, or Old Norse rune poem; the Icelandic rune poem; and the Anglo-Saxon rune poem.

FREY'S AETT: CREATION AND PRODUCTIVITY

Frey is the Norse god of virility, beginnings, and prosperity. The first eight runes of Frey are a journey of creation, from the inception of the cosmos with Fehu, which is associated with Audumla, the primeval cow of Norse mythology, through to gods, giants, light, and bliss, and ending with Wunjo, the gift of the divine order of the universe.

Frey's Aett: Fehu, Uruz, Thurisaz, Ansuz, Raido, Kaunaz, Gebo, Wunjo

HAGALAZ'S AETT: DISRUPTION AND FATE

Hagalaz is the rune of hailstones, so this aett represents disruption. Subject to the laws of nature and the workings of fate, we endure Nauthiz's hardship, Isa's blocks, and the mysteries of the unknown signified by Pertho. With Sowelo, the eighth rune, the sun reappears: We are now in control and empowered.

Hagalaz's Aett: Hagalaz, Nauthiz, Isa, Jera, Eihwaz, Pertho, Algiz, Sowelo

TYR'S AETT: VALUES AND RELATIONSHIPS

Tyr's aett deals with the material world, social values, and relationships. This sequence begins with Tiwaz and Berkana for the male and female principles; Mannaz, for humankind, signifies self-perception and decisions, while Othila is concerned with inheritance, tradition, and order. Like the previous two aetts, Tyr's ends on a high note with Dagaz, rune of optimism and positive change.

Tyr's Aett: Tiwaz, Berkana, Ehwaz, Mannaz, Laguz, Inguz, Othila, Dagaz

Futhark	Origin	Number of runes
The Elder Futhark	Common Germanic	24
The Anglo-Saxon Futhorc	Corth Germanic	29
The Younger Futhark	Scandinavian	16
The Northumbrian runes	Northeast England	33

The oldest Futhark known today is the Elder Futhark, with twenty-four runes. The Younger Futhark is a shortened version of the Elder, while the Anglo-Saxon and Northumbrian Futharks are extensions of the Elder. This chapter illustrates the Elder Futhark.

FREY'S AETT

FEHU

Meaning: Cattle, wealth

Interpretation: Prosperity, value, status, power, creative force

Letter Sound: F

Tarot Cards: III The Empress, IV The Emperor

Inverted Meaning: Financial worries; losing value

Fehu is the rune of material wealth. Kept, sold, or bartered, cattle were a form of currency in Viking society, so this rune also signifies money flowing through trade: negotiation, contracts, and social transactions that bring profit. As wealth accrued often leads to respect and reputation, your professional and personal networks expand and the results you achieve bring positive attention. At home, you may be focused on practical matters: driving a business forward or forging ahead with creative or personal projects. Fehu is associated with Audumbla the Cow, a primordial being in Norse mythology and symbol of abundance.

There is also a sense of accountability with Fehu, as prosperity can mean sacrifices: Is the price you pay for success justified? While you are working hard toward a goal, be sure your investment of time brings you the personal empowerment you desire.

Overall, Fehu brings an opportunity to review and appreciate your achievements. You may share your good fortune with others in the spirit of generous support.

URUZ

Meaning: Aurochs

Interpretation: Strength, courage, resilience, challenges, health, healing

Letter Sound: U

Tarot Card: VIII Strength

Inverted Meaning: Being too domineering; abuse of power

Aurochs are the prehistoric ancestors of modern-day cattle. These huge, cow-like beasts with crescent horns thrived in the forests of Europe largely until the Bronze Age. Uruz, therefore, is the rune of strength and resilience. It represents our primal ability to survive and thrive.

Uruz asks you to live fearlessly, to realize your power to create change, and to react to challenges or opposition with courage and self-belief. The rune can also be reassurance that you will overcome obstacles with patience and standing your ground and by paying close attention to your reactions to conflict. This may mean confronting your fear of failure or of success or overcoming irritation and anger; the battle may be within you. With determination you succeed.

Uruz offers the physical strength of the auroch, so it can reveal a recovery from illness or stress and, overall, signifies vital health and well-being.

THURISAZ

Meaning: Giant

Interpretation: Defense, attack, chaos, protection, resistance

Letter Sound: Th

Tarot Card: XVI The Tower

Inverted Meaning: Irritation rather than upheaval

Thurisaz's traditional meaning is "giant." In Norse mythology, frost giants, or jotun, fought the rule of the gods of Asgard. While the jotun embody a great monster or threat that appears from nowhere, they also represent a challenge to authority. The chaos created may be necessary if profound change is to come.

Thurisaz, therefore, signifies life's disruption—the storms, whirlwinds, or lightning that temporarily turn our world upside down. The rune also invites us to confront this turbulence with courage. It is possible to limit the damage, to guard ourselves from further danger, to protect others in our care, and to fight. You may experience Thurisaz as an attack on your beliefs or a threat to your position or security. As the rune is also associated with the thorn tree, it affords you protection.

Thurisaz can also represent the darker, shadow side of human nature that we suppress and keep out of conscious sight. A secret may come to light.

ANSUZ

Meaning: Ancestor/god

Interpretation: Inspiration, communication, divine intelligence

Letter Sound: A

Tarot Card: I The Magician

Inverted Meaning: Miscommunication

Ansuz is the rune of Odin. The deity of words and communication, he seeks knowledge. His quests demand great sacrifices: He trades an eye for wisdom and must hang from a tree, forgoing all sustenance, before the runes are revealed to him. At a worldly level, the rune therefore suggests that knowledge is not solely about our personal advancement. Words and knowledge are power, and they create conditions for change; as Odin shared his knowledge with mankind, the way we communicate can powerfully affect others and ourselves. In this sense, Ansuz may be using us to express ourselves mindfully. In personal projects, you may be inspired to talk, write, draw, craft, compose, or otherwise manifest ideas. Spiritually, the rune shows you connecting with divine intelligence.

Ansuz represents order and resourcefulness. The rune's meaning of "ancestor" also suggests family connections, ancestral patterns, and past lives. Fehu, the rune of wealth and growth, has two upward strokes, whereas the rune of Ansuz has two downward strokes, suggestive of the past.

RAIDO

Meaning: Ride

Interpretation: Journeys, travel, progress, spiritual path

Letter Sound: R

Tarot Card: VII The Chariot

Inverted Meaning: Procrastination or panic

Raido is the rune of travel. Its meaning is "riding," referring to riding on horseback. In Norse mythology, Sól, the sun, and her brother Máni, the moon, ride across the heavens in horse-drawn chariots, bringing day and night and marking the yearly cycle. They are pursued by terrifying wolves: When the wolves overtake them, the world descends into the chaos of Ragnarok, or the end of a mythic cycle before the world is re-created. The riders must stay on track to maintain the present order.

Raido sees you traveling physically or taking an inner journey, perhaps through spiritual development or through education, discovering new territory, and gaining fresh insights through new experiences. You make progress by taking charge of your journey, moving in the right direction at a pace that is right for you, rather than being led by others' motivations or ego; equally, you may need self-discipline and willpower to stay focused. Overall, this travel rune shows making decisions and taking action toward an important goal.

KAUNAZ (KANO)

Meaning: Torch

Interpretation: Inner wisdom, guidance, knowledge, light

Letter Sound: K or hard C

Element: Fire

Tarot Card: IX The Hermit

Inverted Meaning: Disinterest; ignorance

Kaunaz is the rune of guidance and inner light. It brings intuition, wisdom, and the passing on of knowledge. The Prose Edda, a medieval anthology of verse compiled by Icelandic chief Snorri Sturluson, includes the tale of Odin's theft of the magical mead of poetry, which he shared with chosen gods and mortals. The elixir gave a person poetic inspiration and the ability to answer any question. Odin's quest for knowledge is central to the meaning of Kaunaz: It reveals a personal journey to wisdom through learning and, spiritually, the quest for enlightenment. You may be drawn to teaching, training, or mentoring, or you may otherwise find yourself in a position in which to give advice or to relate history through stories.

Kaunaz can also reveal latent talents and abilities and help you make connections; you may see hidden opportunities or inventive ways to solve a problem. You call upon your intuition and your intellect to find what you are looking for.

GEBO

Meaning: Gift

Interpretation: Gifts, generosity, balance, reciprocity

Letter Sound: G

Tarot Card: XIV Temperance

Inverted Meaning: None

Gebo is the rune of balance and fairness, of giving and receiving in equal measure. It can predict a gift coming to you or show you being generous to others. This may be the giving of time, giving love to a partner or children, or dedicating oneself to a cause. Gebo also asks you to consider the value of balance and equality and to be able not only to give, but to receive gifts with grace, no matter how small. Receiving requires an attitude of surrender, to be comfortable being a passive recipient rather than the active giver.

There is also an aspect of justice in Gebo, in that it speaks of honoring obligations and agreements and committing to what you can reasonably deliver. In this way, the rune supports your need to manage your time, energy, and finances, keeping life in balance. Spiritually, Gebo suggests sacred contracts and karma.

WUNJO

Meaning: Joy

Interpretation: Fulfillment of wishes, blessings, security

Letter Sound: W

Tarot Card: XXI The World

Inverted Meaning: Feeling disconnected

Wunjo, the rune of joy and bliss, brings completion and fulfillment. The Anglo-Saxon rune poem refers to Wunjo as "Bliss he enjoys who knows not suffering, sorrow nor anxiety, | and has prosperity and happiness and a good enough house." This bliss is the appreciation of material and emotional security, rather than the bliss we often associate with spiritual nonattachment. Your hopes and wishes are granted, and your efforts rewarded.

To get to this place of serenity, you may have to overcome great obstacles or endure pressure and frustration. Battles are done, and it is now time to enjoy your successes and share them with others. Wunjo also has the connotation of unity, showing closeness and cooperation in families, friendship groups, and your wider social circles.

HAGALAZ'S AETT

HAGALAZ

Meaning: Hail

Interpretation: Loss or hardship before gain; transformation

Letter Sound: H

Element: Ice

Tarot Cards: XIII Death, X The Wheel of Fortune

Inverted Meaning: None

Hagalaz is the rune of transformation. Its name means "hail," as in a force beyond your control that is disruptive and therefore unwelcome. This is fate, or destiny—the Norse *wyrd* at work. However, the rune asks you to endure hardship because it will lead to positive change; as hail melts into water, a situation will transform over time. Hagalaz advises you to accept the cycles of bad and good fortune, let go of blame, and see the bigger picture beyond day-to-day difficulties. You may also call upon your past experience to help you endure current challenges; you look to your personal history for answers.

The rune is associated with channeling and the underworld realm of the goddess Hel; Hagalaz is also the rune of the mother, so the rune may symbolize the unconscious realm where the dark goddess within us lives. Shadow work or spirit communication may be calling you now. The rune's shape, two parallel lines joined by two strokes, suggests this world and the other-world or the conscious and unconscious selves.

NAUTHIZ

Meaning: Need

Interpretation: Restriction and desire

Letter Sound: N

Element: Fire

Tarot Cards: VI The Lovers, XV The Devil

Inverted Meaning: None

Nauthiz's meaning of "need" suggests "want." When this rune appears in a reading, we may want what we cannot have. We may feel frustrated and restricted: "constraint gives scant choice," says the Old Norwegian rune poem. To make a difficult situation bearable, Nauthiz asks that we live in the present moment and attend to practicalities, an idea expressed in the rune's element of fire.

"Need" also suggests the "need-fires," lit across northern Europe not only to mark the seasons, but as a means of banishing troubles and disease. Villagers lit a communal fire by rubbing flints or two sticks together. Damp wood made the fire give out lots of smoke, and then the cattle, and sometimes the villagers, walked through the smoke, symbolically—and perhaps biologically—curing illness and ending the farmers' misfortune. The runic message here is that lighting a fire with sticks takes work, but you get what you need in the end. An additional meaning of the rune is desire and passion and the need for sex and intimacy.

ISA

Meaning: Ice

Interpretation: Blocks, delay, self-preservation

Letter Sound: I (pronounced *ee*, as in *even*)

Element: Ice

Tarot Card: XII The Hanged Man

Inverted Meaning: None

Isa, the ice rune, represents a blocked or static situation. Water flows, but ice has solid mass and will not melt until conditions change. You may be in control of these conditions, so the rune asks you if you are willing to, for example, look for other routes to your goal. You may need to revise your expectations regarding the timescale of a project or find a way to improve communication in your personal and professional dealings. If this situation is not of your making, use this waiting time as an opportunity for reflection until the blocks dissolve. And there can be value in forced delay; there just might be a gem of an opportunity here that you would otherwise have missed.

Isa also signifies tradition and established values. Ice preserves, and symbolically, it preserves the status quo. If you are trying to break new ground, you may find others resist your desire for change.

JERA

Meaning: Year, harvest

Interpretation: Time, karma, growth, profit

Letter Sound: J or Y

Tarot Card: III The Empress

Inverted Meaning: None

Jera, the twelfth rune in the Elder Futhark sequence, echoes the numbers of the months of the year and hours of the day. In this sense, it is a rune of time. It speaks of right timing—waiting for the right time to push forward and the right time to hold back and rest. This takes experience, patience, and trusting your intuition: to say yes when it feels right to do so, taking on new projects, or embarking on new relationships when you sense a positive energetic flow, rather than assenting to offers because they make logical sense. Everything has its own rhythm, so it is now time to attune to your internal energy so work, love, projects, and finances flow.

The rune is also associated with summer and harvest, when the earth provides for all. This also evokes the concept of karma: reaping what you sow. What you have faithfully invested in will bear fruit in good times.

EIHWAZ (EIWAZ, EITHWAZ)

Meaning: Yew tree

Interpretation: Life cycles, endings, necessary defense

Letter Sound: E (*ay* sound)

Tarot Card: XIII Death

Inverted Meaning: None

Eihwaz, or yew, stands for the ancient, sacred tree that signifies life, death, and rebirth. In this way, the rune speaks of the cycles of nature that we see in trees' budding and falling leaves at the turns of the seasons. Yggrasil, the world tree in Norse mythology, connected the heavens to the earth. This is the focus of Eihwaz—the cycle of life and death, the transition from earth to heaven or spirit. In a reading, the rune can reveal endings and loss that are unavoidable, but we must try to accept them so that new life, or possibilities, can awaken.

Eihwaz is also associated with protection and famed for its hardiness and iron-like wood. Warriors used it to make spears; a yew spear discovered in Essex, Britain, has been dated at around thirteen thousand years old. Eihwaz, therefore, asks you to be mindful of your boundaries and defend yourself physically and spiritually when necessary.

PERTHO (PERTHRO, PERTH)

Meaning: Dice cup

Interpretation: Mysteries, the unknown

Letter Sound: P

Tarot Cards: II The High Priestess, XVIII The Moon

Inverted Meaning: Feeling disempowered or needlessly anxious

Pertho is the rune of mystery. The meaning of "dice cup" signifies divination with dice or runes, which were used by the Vikings to ask questions not only about the harvest and the outcomes of battles, for example, but to inquire about one's personal fate, or orlog. There were two aspects of orlog: the fate that can be changed and the fixed fate that man inherited from his ancestors. Divining the future was not a passive practice; destiny could be changed. Pertho therefore reminds us that outcomes are not fixed. You can change your perceived destiny and see the process of divination as a way to empower yourself with choice. It symbolizes the birth of possibilities and traditionally can also indicate the birth of a child.

Overall, Pertho speaks of the inner self and intuition, the parts of us that become activated by the process of divination. An additional meaning is secrets and the need for discretion, to keep your own counsel and listen to that inner voice.

ALGIZ

Meaning: Elk, elk sedge

Interpretation: Growth, protection, spiritual connection, higher self

Letter Sound: Z

Tarot Card: V The Hierophant

Inverted Meaning: Extreme defensiveness; being too quick to judge or react

We might see Algiz as a human figure raising two arms to the cosmos, an act of worship of the sun or of life—an acknowledgment of the protection and growth that the sun provides. As the next runes in the sequence are Sowelo, sun, and Tiwaz, star, Algiz takes us into higher realms and the higher self. In a rune reading, it can suggest spiritual development, growth, and protection.

Throwing our arms up to the air also suggests surrendering to the forces of nature, staying open to possibilities, and accepting that challenges are a necessary part of our learning.

Other meanings include "elk" and "elk sedge," a type of sharp grass. The grass could wound badly and may account for Algiz's inverted meaning of being overly defensive.

SOWELO (SOWELA, SOWILO)

Meaning: Sun

Interpretation: Success, expansion, power

Letter Sound: S

Element: Fire

Tarot Card: XIX The Sun

Inverted Meaning: None

Sowelo is a rune of optimism and success, bringing the healing and energizing powers of the sun. The sun was revered as the life-giver and the magical will of the Universe: The Norwegian rune poem describes Sol, or Sowelo, as "the light of the world; I bow to the divine decree." The form of Sowelo is a lightning bolt, which connects the sky and the earth. This blast of cosmic power awakens us to our purpose and revitalizes but can also destroy whatever is untrue or

outdated. In a rune-cast, Sowelo says that you will see results.

Spiritually, this rune represents oneness, a feeling of connection with the earth, and being part of a greater whole. Combine the meaning of Sowelo with Raido, ride (see page 50), and we have Raido's willpower aligned with the higher forces and higher self, suggesting powerful personal growth.

TYR'S AETT

TIWAZ (TEIWAZ)

Meaning: Star; the god Tyr

Interpretation: Bravery, tests, justice, victory, guidance

Letter Sound: T

Tarot Cards: XI Justice, XVII The Star

Inverted Meaning: Giving up too soon

Tiwaz is the rune of Tyr or Tiw, god of war and justice. The arrow form of the rune suggests a weapon. In Norse mythology, Tyr sacrificed his sword hand to save the gods. The story implies that there may be no perfect way to win, and we may have to revise our expectations of what success means. Justice in this sense is weighing up the consequences and making a compromise. In a reading, the rune foretells a battle and asks us to look at the process of success: how we get there, rather than winning at any cost.

Tiwaz also means guidance. In the Anglo-Saxon rune poem, this rune is described as "a guiding star," a rune that "is ever on its course over the mists of night and never fails." This tells us to always have hope and self-belief, to keep the faith even when we cannot see the outcome or lose sight of our purpose in the mists of doubt. Support is there.

BERKANA

Meaning: Birch

Interpretation: Beginnings, birth, fertility, growth, creativity, outcomes

Letter Sound: B

Tarot Card: III The Empress

Inverted Meaning: Stuckness; lack of growth; creative blocks

Berkana is the rune of creativity and fertility: giving birth to and nurturing children or creative projects. The Old Norse rune poem says that the birch tree "has the greenest leaves of any shrub," while the Icelandic rune poem associates Berkana with "leafy twig and little tree and fresh young shrub," hence the rune's meaning of fertility and growth. As the birch is also one of the first trees to come into leaf, it represents all spring has to offer: new life, vitality, and possibility.

The rune also means protection; the birch tree was dedicated to Frigga, wife of Odin and protector-goddess of marriage, the home, and the family. She helps love to endure storms and brings peace. When Berkana arrives in a rune-cast, relationships thrive and your projects beautifully unfold.

EHWAZ

Meaning: Horse

Interpretation: Travel, flexibility, cooperation, trust, friendship

Letter Sound: E (short *e* as in *get*)

Tarot Card: VII The Chariot

Inverted Meaning: Misplaced trust

Ehwaz is the travel rune, meaning "horse"; it encompasses all journeys and shows you may take a physical trip. There is a strong spiritual dimension to this rune, as it also indicates shamanic journeying or astral travel. In Norse mythology, Odin rode Sleipnir, his magnificent spirit-horse, from Asgard, realm of the gods, to the realm of the dead. The runes inscribed on Sleipnir's teeth made him invincible on this journey between worlds.

The horse is also a symbol of sexuality, passion, freedom—our primary drives. When Ehwaz arrives in a reading, expressing your basic, instinctual needs may be particularly important. Horses also signify cooperation: Riding a horse requires patience, flexibility, and trust. In this sense, Ehwaz indicates strong, rewarding relationships with others close to you and within the broader community and is a signifier of harmony in your interactions with others.

MANNAZ

Meaning: Mankind

Interpretation: Assessment, decisions, community

Letter Sound: M

Tarot Cards: VI The Lovers, XX Judgment

Inverted Meaning: Narrow-mindedness; hastiness

Mannaz is the rune of discernment, choices, and humankind. It brings perspective and helps us see ourselves and our communities as part of a greater scheme. Humanity also implies a balanced, humane attitude; we may need to forgive or at least be aware of our faults and have compassion for others' shortcomings in the spirit of friendship and support.

The rune's form, which is Wunjo and its mirror image, can signify Wunjo's meaning of "gift" twice: giving and receiving or the give-and-take upon which good relationships depend. Mannaz can also be seen as a progression of Tyr and Berkana, the runes of man and woman.

Ehwaz, the preceding rune, relates to the animal instinct of the horse, whereas Mannaz signifies the reason, or logic, of mankind. In this sense, the rune advises taking a reasoned rather than intuitive approach to a situation. If you have a key decision to make, take a close look at the facts before making a commitment.

LAGUZ

Meaning: Water

Interpretation: Intuition, higher realms, clairvoyance, emotions, collective unconscious

Letter Sound: L

Element: Water

Tarot Cards: II The High Priestess; Queen of Cups

Inverted Meaning: Procrastination; self-doubt

Laguz, meaning "water," is associated with emotions, love, and the flow of life. The rune is a symbol of initiation, perhaps due to the ritual of child naming during the Viking Age: A newborn was held by its father and named, the father sprinkling water on the child as a symbol of welcome. In a rune-cast, Laguz can reveal you are about to experience a new lease of life and perhaps to be initiated into something new.

As a rune of water and psychic ability, Laguz evokes Frigga, wife of Odin and goddess of fertility. Frigga was famed for her clairvoyant ability and shamanic wisdom; she knew the fates of all men and gods but chose to keep this knowledge secret.

Overall, Laguz advises you not to stagnate or hesitate. Immerse yourself in the present, connect with that undercurrent of intuition, and follow it freely.

INGUZ (INGWAZ)

Meaning: The god Ing (Yngvi)

Interpretation: Protection, fertility, development

Letter Sound: Ng (as in sing)

Tarot Card: IV The Emperor

Inverted Meaning: None

The god Ing or Yngvi is identified with Frey, god of fertility and wealth; Ing is likely an older name of the god. In a rune-cast, Ing brings the seeding of ideas, virility, and growth in relationships.

The rune's symmetrical shape indicates completeness and fulfillment; the central diamond suggests containment and protection. Ing's form is the double of Gebo, the rune of gifts—gifts of the earth (sustenance) and the gift of new life (fertility).

Ing also reveals spiritual guidance and balance. The two open triangles at the top and bottom of the rune suggest the same internal space as the inner diamond, showing that the external world of matter is given the same consideration as the inner realm; the conscious and unconscious selves are given equal attention.

OTHILA (OTHALA)

Meaning: Homestead, land

Interpretation: Generations, ancestors, home and family, comfort, stability

Letter Sound: O

Tarot Cards: III The Empress, IV The Emperor

Inverted Meaning: Being stuck in the past; insecurity

Othila is the rune of family and inheritance. This may be what we inherit physically or materially from family, skills or character traits our parents passed on to us, or knowledge we have accrued from the wisdom traditions we follow. When Othila appears in a rune-cast, you may be focusing on home and relationships, feeling a deeper connection with your family and a sense of belonging right where you are. Othila also stands for material wealth. The Othila verse in the Anglo-Saxon rune poem says how a man's territory is precious to him if he enjoys "whatever is right and proper in constant prosperity."

The form of the rune in its upright position is a diamond supported by two crossed sticks: The supports are rooted in the earth, suggesting strong foundations and the protection that material wealth and strong bonds between people bring. In terms of creative projects, the rune shows an idea that is well conceived; in relationships, Othila shows stability and togetherness.

DAGAZ

Meaning: Day

Interpretation: A new start, optimism, realizations

Letter Sound: D

Element: Fire

Tarot Cards: O The Fool, XVII The Star

Inverted Meaning: None

Dagaz represents new beginnings and cycles. The rune's name relates to Dagr, the personification of day in Norse mythology, who traverses the skies on the never-ending journey of day into night. Each day, Dagr rides a chariot pulled by his white horse, Skinfaxi, whose bright mane illuminates the sky and earth. When Dagr sinks and the moon rises, we shift from light to dark, from the conscious to unconscious, from the exterior world to the interior. This twilight time, or period of transition, is associated with heightened awareness and intensity. Spiritually, Dagaz can show awareness of other realities, a cosmic consciousness.

Dagaz also brings hope and improvement, reminding us that "tomorrow is another day." We can start over with renewed optimism. As the Anglo-Saxon rune poem says, Day is "beloved of men, a source of hope and happiness to rich and poor, and of service to all."

Frey's Aett

Rune	Name	Letter	Meaning	Interpretation
ᚠ	Fehu	F	Cattle	Prosperity, value, status
ᚢ	Uruz	U	Aurochs	Strength, courage, resilience
ᚦ	Thurisaz	Th	Giant	Defense, attack
ᚨ	Ansuz	A	God	Inspiration, communication
ᚱ	Raido	R	Ride	Journeys, travel, progress
ᚲ	Kaunaz	K	Torch	Inner wisdom, guidance, knowledge
ᚷ	Gebo	G	Gift	Gifts and generosity
ᚹ	Wunjo	W	Joy	Fulfillment of wishes, blessings

Hagalaz's Aett

Rune	Name	Letter	Meaning	Interpretation
ᚺ	Hagalaz	H	Hail	Loss or hardship before gain
ᚾ	Nauthiz	N	Need	Restriction and desire
ᛁ	Isa	I	Ice	Blocks, delay, self-preservation
ᛃ	Jera	J/Y	Year, harvest	Time, karma, growth, profit
ᛇ	Eihwaz	Ei	Yew	Life cycles, endings, defense
ᛈ	Pertho	P	Dice cup	Mysteries, the unknown
ᛉ	Algiz	Z	Elk, elk sedge	Growth, protection, higher self
ᛊ	Sowelo	S	Sun	Success, expansion, power

Tyr's Aett

Rune	Name	Letter	Meaning	Interpretation
ᛏ	Tiwaz	T	Star, the god Tyr	Bravery, tests, justice, victory, guidance
ᛒ	Berkana	B	Birch	Beginnings, fertility, growth, creativity, outcomes
ᛖ	Ehwaz	E	Horse	Travel, cooperation, trust
ᛗ	Mannaz	M	Mankind	Assessment, decisions, community
ᛚ	Laguz	L	Water	Intuition, clairvoyance, emotions
ᛜ	Inguz	Ng	The god Ing	Protection, fertility, development
ᛟ	Othila	O	Homestead, land	Home and family, comfort, stability
ᛞ	Dagaz	D	Day	New start, optimism, realizations

READING THE RUNES

Before you begin a rune reading, find a clean surface, a white cloth (a symbol of pure intention), and a quiet moment. Prepare yourself as you would for any divination ritual: Take a few deep breaths and try to empty your mind of any distractions. Set the intention that your reading will be for the highest good, and when you are ready, allow your question to form. Then, you have two options:

Place the runes in a set layout. Choose the runes from the bag as you ponder your question and place them in a layout, all faceup. If any are upside down, you can read the inverted and upright meanings.

Cast them onto the cloth. Choose the runes from the bag as you ponder your question and then cast them, letting them gently fall. You interpret the meanings from their positions on the cloth—whether they are in the center or outside, for example. Facedown runes indicate the future.

UPRIGHT AND INVERTED MEANINGS

Some runes have an inverted meaning along with an upright meaning. Noninvertible runes are those that have symmetrical forms, so they look the same upright and inverted. You can read the inverted meaning if the rune falls inverted. However, I advise that you read both the upright and inverted meanings and intuit your own "shadow" meaning, as the inverted meanings alone can be rather direct.

THE THREE NORNS

The Norns were the Norse goddesses of Fate who decided the fates of gods and men. The three runes represent Urd (Wyrd), goddess of the past, Verdandi, goddess of the present, and Skuld, goddess of the future. Traditionally, these three runes are read from right to left, beginning with the future and working backward, but you can intuitively choose to read the runes your own way.

Choose three runes from your bag and place them as shown below.

1	**2**	**3**
Urd:	Verdandi:	Skuld:
The past	The present	The future

THE DECISION READING: **FIVE RUNES**

This layout uses a cross formation and is helpful for decision making, as it examines the issue in detail and offers a rune that represents the lesson that your situation offers.

Choose five runes from your bag and place them as shown below:

3
What supports you

2
Potential challenges

5
The final outcome and the lesson learned

4
The immediate outcome

1
The influence of the past

THE **NINE-RUNE** CAST

This is a free-form reading, in which you choose nine runes randomly from the bag and gently drop them onto a white cloth or surface. If any fall facedown, leave them until the end of the reading, as these represent the future.

First, look at the runes in the center of the cloth. These represent priorities—the issues or situations that are important to you now—and can reveal hidden influences that may be affecting you.

Secondly, look at any runes that have fallen near the edges of the cloth. These represent how other people may be influencing you or your

situation. (Ignore any runes that lie outside the area of your cloth, as they represent things that have little influence upon you just now.)

Finally, look at the facedown runes, turning them faceup but keeping them in the same position on the cloth. These represent the future.

Now, look at how the runes in your reading form small groups. Interpret these groups together. It's also helpful to look up the elements associated with some runes on pages 48 through 59. For example, if a fire rune and an ice rune were close to one another, this suggests tension, given that ice and fire are elemental opposites.

THE **GRID OF DESTINY**

This reading is a development of the past, present, future method of the three Norns (see page 61), showing you the influence of friends and family, and it includes a rune that reveals the spiritual perspective on your situation.

If you are reading for another person, he or she chooses eight runes from the bag, and you, as the reader, choose the ninth.

7
Spiritual matters

8
Friends

9
Outcome. Chosen by the rune master or mistress.

4
The past

5
Family

6
What helps or hinders you

1
The Significator. Represents you or the querent.

2
Inner self

3
Goals

The runes of the Elder Futhark also represent the calendar year. You can refer to the rune of your birth for insights into your personality.

Each of the twenty-four Elder Futhark runes governs two weeks of the year, and each rune also rules one hour of the day, so you can identify a second rune that represents the time of your birth. Your day and hour of birth runes are interpreted together to give a character reading:

Birthday rune: The external, or how you are perceived. What you show to the world; qualities and skills you share; how you consciously regard yourself.

Hour rune: The internal, or your inner self. What you hide; inner qualities; attitudes you may be less conscious of.

You may get the same rune for your birthday and hour of birth, in which case there is alignment between your inner and outer selves. You have a strong personality and your motivation is clear.

Each rune's two-week influence begins and ends at 12:30 p.m. Fehu, for example, begins at 12:30 p.m. on June 29 and ends at 12:30 p.m. on July 14. If you were born on a changeover day, you will need to know your time of birth to find your runic sign. If you do not know your birth time, interpret the two runes that cover your day.

Rune	Runic Hour	Runic Fortnight
Frey's Aett		
Fehu	12:30 p.m.–1:30 p.m.	June 29–July 14 (Herb harvest)
Uruz	1:30 p.m.–2:30 p.m.	July 14–29
Thurisaz	2:30 p.m.–3:30 p.m.	July 29–August 14
Ansuz	3:30 p.m.–4:30 p.m.	August 14–29
Raido	4:30 p.m.–5:30 p.m.	August 29–September 13
Kaunaz	5:30 p.m.–6:30 p.m.	September 13–28 (Autumn equinox)
Gebo	6:30 p.m.–7:30 p.m.	September 28–October 13
Wunjo	7:30 p.m.–8:30 p.m.	October 13–28
Hagalaz's Aett		
Hagalaz	8:30 p.m.–9:30 p.m.	October 28–November 13 (Halloween)
Nauthiz	9:30 p.m.–10:30 p.m.	November 13–28
Isa	10:30 p.m.–11:30 p.m.	November 28–December 13
Jera	11:30 p.m.–12:30 a.m.	December 13–28 (Winter solstice)
Eihwaz	12:30 a.m.–1:30 a.m.	December 28–January 13
Pertho	1:30 a.m.–2:30 a.m.	January 13–28
Algiz	2:30 a.m.–3:30 a.m.	January 28–February 12
Sowelo	3:30 a.m.–4:30 a.m.	February 12–27
Tyr's Aett		
Tiwaz	4:30 a.m.–5:30 a.m.	February 27–March 14
Berkana	5:30 a.m.–6:30 a.m.	March 14–30 (Spring equinox)
Ehwaz	6:30 a.m.–7:30 a.m.	March 30–April 14
Mannaz	7:30 a.m.–8:30 a.m.	April 14–29
Laguz	8:30 a.m.–9:30 a.m.	April 29–May 14 (May Day)
Inguz	9:30 a.m.–10:30 a.m.	May 14–29
Othila	10:30 a.m.–11:30 a.m.	May 29–June 14
Dagaz	11:30 a.m.–12:30 p.m.	June 14–29 (Summer solstice)

3 READING THE TRACES

TEA, COFFEE, AND SALT

From the oracles of the ancients, we move into the domestic sphere and the kitchen table: to tasseomancy and salt readings, the techniques of our more recent ancestors. To read teacups, coffee cups, and salt, we interpret what is left behind when the ceremonial sipping or sifting is done; in the traces, we may see symbols, marks, and patterns that offer insights into our past, present, and future.

FORTUNE-TELLING IN A TEACUP

Tasseomancy, which means "cup" and "divination," embraces both tea leaf reading and reading coffee grounds. Legend has it that a leaf infusion was the accidental discovery of Chinese Emperor Shen Nong in 2737 BCE. By the seventeenth century, European countries were importing tea from Asia. By the Victorian era, tea drinking had become a social ritual and tea leaf reading became a parlor game.

Tea leaf reading has thrived as a divinatory art not only because its popularity testifies to our thirst for fortune-telling, but because the ritual of tea drinking is so embedded in our culture; it's an art we can practice around the kitchen table without the need for crystal balls or cards. This practice has been handed down from mother to daughter, an unwritten wisdom that in some families has become an honored tradition.

HOW TO
READ YOUR TEA LEAVES

Before you begin, let go of any pressure to give specific predictions or answers for yourself or others. Look at the time you'll take to make tea, drink, and interpret the symbols in your cup as an opportunity to free your intuition and open up to imaginative possibilities. Explore the patterns of the leaves at your leisure and see what takes shape; you don't need to see a unicorn in your cup for your reading to be magical—a few dots, lines, or curves can tell you much about present and future influences.

Choose a large white or light-colored teacup with a saucer. A bowl-shaped one is better than a straight-sided mug, as you'll be able to see the distribution of the leaves more easily. You'll need fresh, loose tea—traditional or herbal—or you can tear open a tea bag and use the contents, but ensure that the tea isn't dust-like and old. You'll be drinking the tea with some small leaves in it. It's fine to add milk; milk won't affect the reading.

Think about your question and make your tea in a pot or put one teaspoon of tea in your teacup and add boiling water. Leave it to brew for 3 to 4 minutes to allow the leaves to settle on the bottom of the cup.

When you've poured your tea from the pot or you're ready to drink your cup-made tea, stop and look at the surface of the liquid. Refer to the chart on the left to determine the meaning of the bubbles.

Drink your tea, leaving some liquid in the bottom. If you prefer, pour out some of the tea rather than drink it, so around two teaspoons of liquid are left. You'll need enough liquid in the cup to swirl the residual leaves.

Next, hold the cup in your left hand and swirl it counterclockwise three times, while thinking of your question or the life area you'd like to know about. Then, slowly invert the cup on the saucer so the remaining liquid drains out. Leave the cup inverted for a minute or two. Then, turn the cup the right way up and hold it in your right hand. You're ready to read the pattern of tea leaves inside it.

Bubbles on the surface at the side of the cup	}	Future love
Bubbles swirling in the center:	}	Money coming. The more bubbles, the more money.
A whole single tea leaf, floating	}	A visitor; a stranger

ALTERNATIVE METHOD

If you can't abide the strong taste of tea in the bottom of the cup, try this: Pour the tea from the pot through a tea strainer and interpret any bubbles on the surface. Then, hold the tea strainer over an empty cup. Tap the strainer once, sharply, so the leaves fall into the cup, and then follow the instructions below.

HOW TO INTERPRET YOUR CUP

Begin by holding the cup with the handle toward you. See where the leaves are distributed; the area immediately below the handle represents you and your situation, so anything on the inside of the cup close to the handle is directly relevant to you. The region opposite the handle reveals what's away from you—people or events happening at a physical distance.

1 Examine the fall of the leaves. In folk tradition, evenly dispersed leaves were considered a good cup, while many leaves at the bottom of the cup were considered less fortunate.

2 Look at the leaf patterns. What marks and symbols do you see? Now, turn the cup so you can see symbols from another angle. You may start with a bird and end with the initial M, for example. Take your time finding the symbols and let them evolve. You can intuit their meanings if you're familiar with symbols or refer to the symbol interpretations on page 74.

3 How large are the marks or symbols? The bigger the symbol and the clearer it is, the more important the event or influence. If you see a number in your cup, take note, as this gives you a timescale for your reading (see "Timing Methods," on the following page).

4 Where do the symbols fall? The location of the symbols can modify their meaning. The rim and top area of the cup traditionally denote happiness, whereas the bottom of the cup represents unhappy events. So, if you were to get a good-fortune symbol near the rim, the symbol's location increases its positive message. A good-fortune symbol around the bottom of the cup dilutes some of the symbol's positivity. Likewise, a negative symbol around the top and rim means that the negative influence is short-lived.

The Location of Events

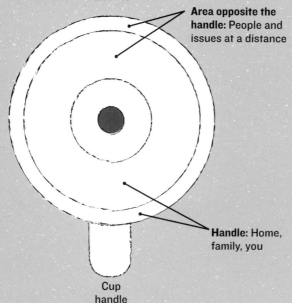

Area opposite the handle: People and issues at a distance

Handle: Home, family, you

Cup handle

TIMING METHODS

Timing is an issue in every divinatory practice. If we consider that tea leaf reading is all about the future and opening up to possibilities so that the future can flow, precise timing becomes unimportant. If, however, you or a client has a specific question about an event that's time-sensitive, there are several methods here to guide you.

1 The simple method: Look at the rim to the base as a timeline, with symbols at the rim and top showing the present and immediate future in days; symbols in the middle of the cup in weeks; and symbols in the lower part of the cup in one or more months ahead. So, the lower the leaves in the cup, the further into the future we go.

2 There's also a nice layer of interpretation for spiritual and emotional insights (shown in gray in the illustration). The rim and top denote what you're consciously aware of—these are known issues and people. The middle of the cup shows what's emerging, what you might be processing internally, perhaps through dreams. Symbols at the lower and base of the cup can reveal buried issues and seeds of new possibilities.

3 Using the twelve sectors: Imagine the cup is divided into twelve sectors, like a wheel. Starting from the left of the handle, we begin with one month ahead, moving clockwise up to eleven months. If a symbol is in sector 7, for example, the prediction would be that this event will happen seven months from now. The difficulty with this technique is that you need a large cup and to be able to imagine the sector in which a symbol lies; if you're new to teacup reading, you may prefer to use the simple method of timing and focus on symbol interpretation rather than month-to-month timing.

4 Numbers as days, weeks, or months: If you see a number in your cup, it's a sign of timing. A number near the top of the cup would indicate days, the middle of the cup would indicate weeks, and the lower area and base would indicate months. However, use your intuition, too; if the number is large and obvious, you may sense that this implies immediacy, regardless of where it falls in the cup.

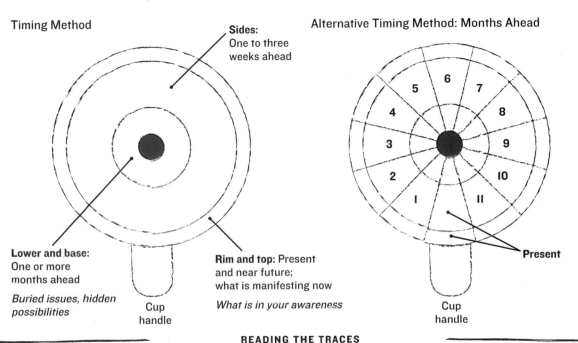

Timing Method

Sides:
One to three weeks ahead

Lower and base:
One or more months ahead

Buried issues, hidden possibilities

Cup handle

Rim and top: Present and near future; what is manifesting now

What is in your awareness

Alternative Timing Method: Months Ahead

5 6 7
4   8
3   9
2   10
1   11

Present

Cup handle

WHAT ABOUT **THE PAST?**

You may wish to ignore the past entirely when you read tea leaves, as this time-honored art is traditionally used to predict the future. However, some readers see the right-hand side of the cup as the future and the left-hand side as the past, with the present located around and opposite the handle (in the areas of home and away in the illustration on the previous page). So to read the future in a cup, you would hold the cup with the handle toward you and look at the symbols to the right of the handle. The top and rim down to the base is your timeline, running from near future (days) to distant future (months) at the bottom. For example, if you see a ring symbol to the right of the handle in the middle area, this would mean a love commitment coming within the next few weeks.

READING **THE SAUCER**

If you have any residual leaves on the saucer, you can read them. Saucer reading is helpful if you feel the cup hasn't given you enough to go on, but otherwise, it often validates the predictions found in the cup.

The center of the saucer represents you and immediate events affecting you. The next ring around you reveals events to come in the next few weeks, while the outer ring and rim show more distant events, usually one month or more into the future.

TEA LEAF **SYMBOLS**

There is a common thread of meaning between leaf symbols and dream symbols, so the symbols given here can be read as psychic symbols that may appear in, for example, dreams, mirrors, crystals, or water during scrying.

Acorn: Financial luck and good health.

Airplane: Unexpected travel; seeing from a higher perspective.

Anchor: Good luck and stability.

▸ **At the top of the cup:** good relationships and business achievement.

▸ **In the middle or bottom of the cup:** a journey leading to money.

Angel: Love and good news; guidance and protection.

Ant: Strategy, hard work.

Apple: Discovery; the pursuit of knowledge; good health.

Arc: A need to get complete with a relationship or project that is currently on hold.

Arrow: Unwelcome news; criticism or aggression.

▸ **Pointing toward the cup handle:** the aggression is directed at you.

▸ **Pointing away from the handle:** you are the initiator.

Axe: Challenges.

Bag: Restriction; the need to think several steps ahead and expect underhandedness.

Ball: Going with flow; accepting ups and downs.

Balloon: Unexpected improvement.

Barrel: Focus on actions; time to move ahead rather than talk about it.

Bat: Choose your friends carefully.

Bear: Challenging territory ahead.

▸ **Facing away from the cup handle:** a long journey.

Bed: Good organization and happiness.

Bee: Good news; hard work brings money and success; blessings.

▸ **Near the cup handle:** parties and happy gatherings.

▸ **Swarm of bees:** good fortune results from a group situation, such as a meeting.

Bell: A result or declaration; look for other symbols nearby to see if this is favorable.

▸ **At the top of the cup:** promotion.

▸ **Two bells:** a prosperous marriage; success.

Birds: Good news and journeys. See also Raven.

Boat: A short trip or help during stress; a place or time for recuperation.

▸ **At the bottom of the cup:** if the boat is overturned, trust issues.

Book: Knowledge.

▸ **Open book:** education or a lawsuit.

▸ **Closed book:** spiritual development or hidden knowledge.

Boomerang: Karma; what goes around, comes around.

Boot: Good fortune and protection.

Bow: Hope and self-expression; expanding horizons.

Bracelet: Partnership.

Bridge: You find a fast route to success.

73

Broom: The way ahead is clear; minor irritations disappear.

Bull: Success in negotiations; strength of character and good health.

Butterfly: Fun and socializing; charm and charisma.

▶ **Surrounded by dots:** money worries due to overspending.

Caduceus: Healing and money.

▶ **Near the cup handle:** an important letter.

Cage: Restriction.

Cake: Celebrations, parties.

Camel: A responsibility; this may involve traveling.

Candle: Generosity and inspiring others.

Cart: Transactions selling a house, receiving a legacy, or benefiting from a business deal.

Castle: A high position, but can warn against arrogance.

Cat: Hidden opposition; someone may not be trustworthy.

Cell phone: Messages, news.

Circle or ring: Good fortune, love and commitment, success.

▶ **Broken by a line:** separation.

Chain: Established, successful relationships.

▶ **Broken:** Breakup in a relationship or business agreement.

Chair: Stability; improvement at work.

▶ **Surrounded by dots:** more money.

Chimney: Being of service to others.

Circle: Everything goes well; successful completion.

Claw: Protect your reputation and possessions.

Cloak: Lack of clarity; delay any commitments, such as signing papers.

Clock: Do what you need to do now; don't procrastinate.

Clouds: Doubt and irritation, soon passing.

Clover leaf: Luck, particularly if a four-leaf clover.

▶ **At the top of the cup:** immediate success.

Coil: Confusion; the need to unravel a situation.

Coin: An agreement brings in money.

Column: High achievement.

Comma: Temporary rest.

▶ **Several commas:** procrastination.

Corn: Abundance.

Cow: Prosperity, growth, and happiness.

Cross: You may need to make a sacrifice to move on.

Crow: See Raven.

Crown: Trust and authority; being valued.

Cup: Rewards.

▶ **With dots around it:** financial reward.

Deer: Unexpected news; other symbols close to the deer will offer further insights.

Dog: Faithful friendship.

▸ **At the bottom of the cup:** a friend needs you.

Dot: Emphasizes the symbol next to it. See also Butterfly, Chair, Cup, Knife, Letter.

Dove: Harmony at home.

Dragon: A profound change that feels dangerous but is ultimately empowering.

Duck: Profit.

Eagle: Leadership and protection; also, a symbol of the father.

Ear: Keep your own counsel and ignore rumors.

Egg: Beginnings, creativity, fertility, and productivity.

▸ **Near the cup handle:** a baby coming into the family.

Elephant: Wisdom and determination; patience and hard work bring success.

Eye: Insight and perception; you may need to supervise a situation closely.

Eyeglasses: An unexpected discovery.

Fairy: Romance and adventures; imagination and creativity.

Feather: Angelic guidance.

Fence: The need to set boundaries or feeling limited by them.

Fern: Uncertainty.

Fir tree: Success and influence.

Fire: Anger, outbursts.

Fish: Abundance, money, luck, and success.

Flower: A wish granted.

Fly: Temporary irritations; minor problems at home.

Fork: Decisions; look for other symbols close by for guidance.

Fox: Betrayal and disloyalty; you may need to observe others closely and be vigilant.

Frog: A new home; also, a need for humility.

Grapes: Abundance; indulgence.

Guitar: Love, attraction, and harmony.

Hammer: Focus; determination.

Hand: A new friendship and success.

Harp: Serenity, socializing, and new friends; in love, a happy partnership.

Heart: Love and happiness.

▸ **Two hearts close together:** commitment, such as marriage.

Hill: A test.

Horse: Serving others; loyalty and wisdom.

Horseshoe: Good luck; make the most of this opportunity.

House: Stability; good conditions for success at work.

▸ **At the top of the cup:** moving home.

Human figure: A visitor.

Insect: Worries. See also specific insects Ant, Fly.

Ivy: Reliable friends and support.

▸ **Near the cup handle:** a faithful lover.

Jewel: A gift.

Jug: Generosity; supporting others.

Key: New opportunities; strategies for success; unlocking secrets.

Kite: Ambition; holding on to your goals.

Knife: Disagreement; separation.

▸ **Surrounded by dots:** arguments about money.

Ladder: Clear goals and commitment.

Lantern: The light within; inner knowing and protection.

Leaf: News.

▸ **If more than one leaf:** happiness and success.

Letter: News; look to see if there is an initial letter close to this symbol, as this can show who the letter, email, or text might be from.

▸ **If the letter symbol is surrounded by dots:** news about money.

Letters of the alphabet: Initials of a person or people.

Lily: Purity and integrity; honest, clear communication.

Lines, crossed: Decisions to be made.

Lion: Honors and awards.

Lock: An obstacle; projects delayed.

Log: Stuckness; low energy.

Mermaid: Imagination, but also illusion and temptation; an offer may not be substantial.

Monkey: Mischief; playfulness.

Moon: A full moon means happiness and love coming.

▸ **If a crescent moon, waxing:** new projects and growth.

▸ **If a crescent moon, waning:** decrease in interest; wait for a better time.

Mountain: Ambition and reward.

▸ **If the mountain has lines across it:** challenges to be overcome.

Mouse: Lack of funds; the need to be more proactive.

Mushroom: Sudden growth or improvement.

▸ **Shown near a heart:** romance; may need to take it slowly.

Musical note: Good luck.

Necklace: Love and relationships are important now; if the necklace is intact, love is stable; if broken, this suggests a breakup.

Net: Falling into a trap or netting a prize; proceed carefully.

Numbers: Gives a timescale (days, weeks, months).

Oak: Health and prosperity; others rely on your strength.

Owl: Wisdom, but also caution; pay attention to detail.

Palm tree: Honors, success, and respect.

Pan: Self-containment; the need to break out of routines.

Parrot: Gossip.

Pear: Reward for hard work; money flows; material comforts.

Pentagon: Good organization brings success.

Piano, piano keys: Peace and harmony.

Pig: Finding a balance between satisfaction and greed.

Pyramid: Past lives; origins and identity; spiritual development.

Question mark: You question your abilities or your intuition; a decision needs to be made.

Rabbit: Sensitivity and fertility; escaping problems that need to be addressed.

Rainbow: Hope and optimism.

Rat: Survival; you may need to act out of character to outwit an opponent.

Raven or crow: The need to find your life purpose; feeling unsettled and seeking stability.

Reptile: Intense emotions such as anger, guilt, or envy.

Ring: Completion, love, and friendship.

Road: The unknown future; new opportunities.

Rose: Affection, friendship, joy, and success.

Scales: Justice and decisions.

▶ **If the scales are balanced:** you will be treated fairly.

▶ **If the scales are unbalanced:** a decision goes against you.

Scissors: Misunderstandings and arguments.

Scythe: Sudden endings that are unavoidable; seeing the truth.

Shark: Opposition; the need to show your strength.

Sheep: A wake-up call to speak up rather than follow a group consensus.

Shell: Inner wisdom and guidance.

Ship: A well-defined ship brings prosperity and health; if broken and ill-formed, disappointment.

▶ **If there are two or more ships:** a successful commercial venture. See also Boat.

Snail: A slow, steady approach; this may be comfortable but not bring you timely results.

Snake: Wisdom and renewal, or mistrust; look at the surrounding symbols for further guidance.

Spade: Success comes from hard, consistent work.

Spider: Inventiveness, but the danger of over-complicating what could be a simpler task; networks, news, and communication.

Spiral: A slow but steady rise to fame.

Spoon: A christening.

▶ **If two spoons:** a fun flirtation.

Square: Restriction or protection; look to the surrounding symbols for further guidance.

Stairs: Improvement; spiritual development.

Star: Happiness and good fortune; wishes come true.

Sun: Empowerment and happiness; others are drawn to you.

Swan: Advancement.

▶ **If flying:** money coming.

Sword: Opposition and challenges to your position.

Table: Eating and socializing.

Teapot: Meetings and discussions; being asked for input.

Telescope: Foresight; seeing beyond the present.

Tiger: Prosperity; fierce attraction in relationships; aggressive tactics.

Tortoise: Slow progress and slow success.

Tower: The past; a discovery connected with the past shines a new light on the present.

Train: Expanding horizons; events speed up.

Trees: Strength and growth, shelter and care; the family. See also Oak.

Triangle: Success.

▶ **Downward-pointing:** disappointment.

Trowel: Patient attention to detail now assures future success.

Umbrella: Protection.

Unicorn: Spiritual connection; imagination, art, magic, and creativity.

Vase: Being of service to others; sharing your gifts.

Violin: Following your own path; independence.

Volcano: Suppressed emotion.

Wasp: Being stung; hurtful actions or comments.

Web: Intrigue; being caught up in an unexpected situation; take good advice.

Whale: The ability to make a success of a great project.

Wheel: Change and progress.

Wing: Messages. See also Angel.

Wolf: Instinct; the need to fight for or protect others.

Zebra: A nomadic lifestyle or a trip overseas; a secret affair.

COFFEE CUP READINGS

The Turkish tradition of divining with coffee grounds dates to the sixteenth century and the introduction of coffee as trade and social ritual under the Ottoman Empire. The Turkish proverb "A single cup of coffee commits one to forty years of friendship" not only confirms the cultural importance of coffee, but may be the origin of the timescale given in traditional coffee cup readings: The cup sees forty days into the future.

PREPARATION

You will need Turkish or Greek coffee (finely ground arabica beans) plus white or cream-colored demitasse cups and saucers (a demitasse is a small cup that holds around 2.5 fl oz or 75 ml of liquid); white or light-colored china or earthenware gives the best contrast to the muddy-brown coffee grounds. The saucer is a key component because the cup is inverted on it to drain off any remaining liquid before a reading, and you can interpret the residue on the saucer, too, after you have read the cup. Traditionally, Turkish coffee is made in a cezve—a small copper or brass pot with a straight handle. These are widely available online, but as an alternative, you can make your coffee in a regular pan.

THE COFFEE RECIPE:
FOR TWO CUPS

Use one of the demitasse cups you are going to drink from to measure the water; for two people, pour two cups of water into a cezve or pan. Add three heaped teaspoons of finely ground coffee (more if you like strong coffee). If you take sugar, add it. Stir with a spoon and then heat it close to a boil; you'll see a thick, frothy foam (but don't let the coffee boil, which will give it a bitter taste). Remove from the heat and put some of the foam into each cup. Then repeat, so you've frothed the coffee twice. Pour into cups. If you're using a pan rather than a cezve, stir the coffee as you pour from pan to cup to ensure the sediment doesn't remain in the pan.

READING THE CUP AND SAUCER

When the coffee is cooled, sip it, drinking from only one side of the cup. Leave a few sips in the cup.

1 Ask your question or just ask to see what's important for you now. Place the saucer over the top of the cup so the cup is covered and won't spill, as you are about to swirl it. Now, hold the cup and saucer and swirl it around three times to the right. Keeping the cup and saucer together, invert them, so the cup is upside down on the saucer. Place it on a surface and leave for around ten minutes to cool and drain.

2 Next, separate the cup and saucer.

3 If you cannot separate them without some effort, this means that you have no need for a reading; everything is as it should be.

4 If big chunks of coffee grounds fall out of the cup into the saucer, all your troubles will soon be gone.

5 If coffee drips onto the saucer as you're lifting the cup from it, tears will fall.

6 Hold the cup with the handle toward you, ready to begin your reading. Follow the instructions for teacup reading on page 70 and see the symbols list on page 74.

7 Look at the saucer: If it contains a lot of liquid, tip it into the cup (which you're now finished with) to reveal a pattern of sediment on the saucer. Often, the saucer markings support the meanings of those seen in the cup, so if you are unsure of anything you've seen in the cup, the saucer often clarifies this. For example, if you saw the vague shape of a bird near the rim of your cup, showing the possibility of an imminent journey, birds in the saucer confirm the prediction: Your trip will happen.

SALT READINGS

Alomancy, also known as halomancy, means divination by means of salt. Salt is used widely in spiritual cleansing and protection rituals, and it has symbolic meaning. Its importance in ritual may have been reinforced by its cost. Expensive to produce before industrialization, salt was a precious commodity—which may explain why spilled salt was regarded as an omen of quarrels or bad luck to come.

Salt reading, like tea leaf reading and hydromancy (see pages 68 and 213), requires only what you have in your kitchen. You can use regular table salt.

SALT-CASTING

You will need salt and a small black skillet. As an alternative to the pan, you could use a dark plate, baking sheet, or cake tin; any surface will do, provided it is dark and flat.

Take a handful of salt. Take a slow breath in and out and ask your question (e.g., "Will *x* project go well? Will I get *x* opportunity?") or simply ask the salt to show what you need to know just now. Holding the salt above the pan, close your eyes and scatter it into the pan, keeping your question or request in mind. You might find you sprinkle it or release it in bursts; just do what

feels right in the moment. Alternatively, you can pour the salt from its container—hold it upright over the pan, close your eyes, ask your question, and then tip it for a second or two so your salt is cast and ready to read.

INTERPRETING YOUR SALT

Ridges: Challenges; obstacles.

Undulations: Slowness; delays to your plans; start-stop.

A small well: Protection; relief from stress.

Swirls on the right of the pan: Manifesting. A situation is progressing; an idea is incubating. You are moving toward your wish.

Swirls on the left of the pan: The need to let go. A time of transition.

If you see other shapes or numbers in the salt, interpret them as you would a teacup, using the list of symbols on page 74.

ALTERNATIVE METHOD: ALEUROMANCY

As an alternative to salt, you can use flour. Flour divination, or aleuromancy, is an ancient form of divination. Predictions were written on slips of paper and placed inside a dough ball, much like fortune cookies today. To use flour in the same way as salt, follow the salt method: Take a handful of flour, ask your question, and release the flour onto a dark plate, pan, or other surface. Refer to the salt interpretations above.

4 PALMISTRY

READING THE LINES

Palmistry is one of the most time-honored divination techniques. It may seem complex; there are many lines, marks, and symbols on the hand, and professional palmists spend years studying their meanings. However, much can be gleaned from just one or two features of the hand or palm, so a basic understanding, coupled with your intuition, will help you begin reading sooner than you thought possible.

PALMISTRY ORIGINS

Palmistry is believed to have its roots in the traditions of the Roma travelers (gypsies) and in ancient India, with the Hindu poet Valmiki's *The Teachings of Valmiki Maharshi on Male Palmistry*. From India, palmistry spread to China, Tibet, Egypt, Persia, Greece, and other European countries.

The publication of Casimir Stanislas D'Arpentigny's book *La Chirognomie* (1839) was instrumental in reviving interest in palmistry after its suppression during the Middle Ages. More books followed, including those by society palmist Cheiro (William John Warner; 1866–1936). One of the world's most renowned seers, Cheiro received the Order of the Lion and the Star from the Shah of Persia in 1900 as a reward for warning him of an assassination attempt. Reading for many significant people, from Mark Twain to Oscar Wilde to the Prince of Wales, Cheiro brought increased attention to palmistry, and it has remained popular since.

THE NOT-SO-FIXED FUTURES OF PALMISTRY

Because we're examining the physical body for clues, rather than looking at tea leaves or tarot cards which change with every reading, there can be an assumption that palmistry is fatalistic: It deals with fixed lines, so must deal in fixed futures. Yet the lines on your hand can and do change over time so, like any other divination method, a palm-reading reflects where you are now in your life.

LEARNING TO READ THE HAND AND THE PALM

One of palmistry's great appeals is its ability to show timings because all the major lines are divided into time segments. So, when you feel confident reading the lines, interpret the timings. You'll be amazed at how accurately a hand records past events and emotions.

Palmistry also has much to say about health. However, our role as would-be palmists is not to diagnose or predict health issues; seeing one in the future does not mean it is unavoidable. If health comes up in the interpretations in this chapter, it is expressed in general terms—for example, being prone to illness or stress.

Palmistry has two aspects: chirognomy and chiromancy. Chirognomy means reading the shape and qualities of the hand (for example, gaps between fingers, the skin's texture, and joints). Chiromancy is the interpretation of the lines and other markings. You can use chirognomy, chiromancy, or both to get information. Begin with chirognomy and practice reading on yourself and others. If you're feeling overwhelmed, just focus on one aspect—you can learn a lot about a person from the length of and shape of the thumb, for example. When you are comfortable, you'll have a template on which to explore chiromancy.

HOW THE LINES CHANGE OVER TIME

The lines on the palm can change over a two- to three-month period. Some believe that they change in accordance with our free will, reflecting our thoughts and actions. If you regularly take palm prints (see page 103), you're potentially able to see, in your right hand, what you are manifesting. A reading can also help pinpoint opportunitles or danger points in the future. Armed with this knowledge, the person has a choice—to keep going along the same track or make decisions that will create an alternative outcome.

LEFT- AND RIGHT-HAND **MEANINGS**

If you are right-handed, your right, or active, hand shows how you're using your abilities; the left, or passive, hand shows the abilities you were born with. If you are left-handed, the reverse is true. For the purposes of this chapter, I refer to the right hand as dominant.

A palmist looks at both the left and right hands, but focuses mainly on the right hand during the reading because this hand tells you what you are manifesting, and have manifested, in your life now. He or she may refer to the left hand to see if you were born with a particular character trait or talent, and by comparing features and markings on the two hands, you can see if this is something you've developed. Comparing both hands is important, as it also reveals your future potential. For example, the palmist might see a well-developed mount of Mercury until the little finger of your left hand and a flattish corresponding mount on your right hand. This shows that you have a natural ability to write and communicate that you're not yet using—an observation that offers a deeper realization of your special abilities.

Note how the lines on the hand can differ; there can also be differences in the size of the fingers and mounts (see pages 94 and 97).

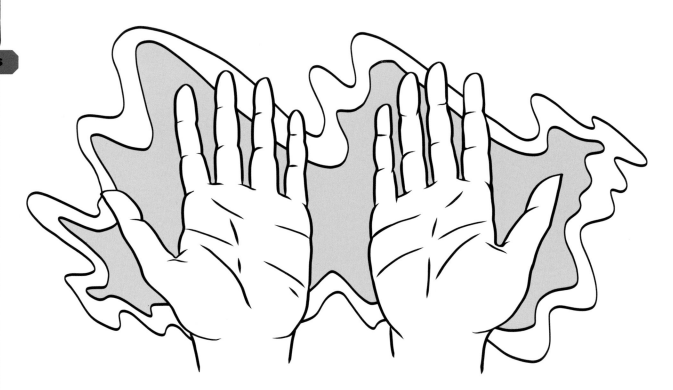

Left (passive) hand: Reveals inherited traits; early and family influences; your destiny.

Right (active) hand: Reveals if you are using or overlooking your natural abilities.

CHIROGNOMY

Chirognomy refers to the shape and qualities of the hand—the shape of the palm, fingers, and thumbs; fingertip markings and nail shape; finger gaps; the prominence of joints; and the skin's texture, for example.

HAND POSITION, TEXTURE, AND COLOR

First, look at the natural hand position. Try it on your own hand:

Turn your hand palm upward and rest your hand comfortably on a flat surface or in your lap. Find a position that feels natural.

1 If your thumb is away from your hand and does not touch any of your fingers, you have an open hand. (It's likely that all or some of the fingers will be open, too.) This reveals an open character; you're open to ideas and opportunities, are willing to take some risks, and tend to be generous. If your thumb rests against or touches one of your fingers, this denotes a closed hand; you have a more cautious attitude to money and risk-taking, along with a need for privacy and discernment.

2 Now, look at the angle the thumb makes with the side of the hand:

Less than 45 degrees from the side of the hand: Closed, conservative nature.

45 to 90 degrees: Considered average—a balanced, open nature.

More than 90 degrees: Leadership qualities, but can be impetuous and headstrong.

Skin texture can also form a part of the reading, as it can denote health and temperament. It's believed that a pale palm can show anemia and a reddish palm might indicate high blood pressure. Coarse, rough skin might indicate a practical person, while fine, smooth skin is a sign of sensitivity. However, these meanings seem more logical deduction than divination, and health indicators may not be appropriate in a reading, so use your discretion; the hand position often says more than color and texture.

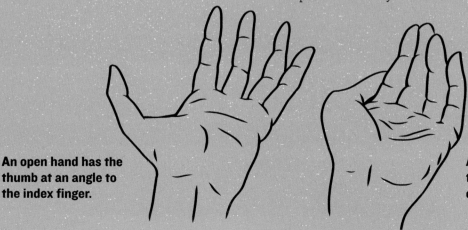

An open hand has the thumb at an angle to the index finger.

A closed hand has the thumb touching one of the fingers.

HAND **SHAPES**

The classification of six hand shapes, plus a "mixed" hand, came to us from Casimir Stanislas D'Arpentigny in his book *La Chirognomie* (1839). These shapes were geared for reading male hands: the elemental, spatulate, and square hands, for example, are related to broad or square palms and stubby or bulbous fingertips.

The original descriptions often overlap, hence the inclusion of a mixed hand type. They are included here for your reference. Modern palmistry now opts for the four elemental hand shapes, linking hand shape to Earth, Air, Fire, or Water, an idea proposed by the British palmist Fred Gettings in *The Book of the Hand* (1965).

The Six Traditional Hand Shapes

If you have a mixture of hand types, read the interpretations that relate to the hand types that most reflect yours.

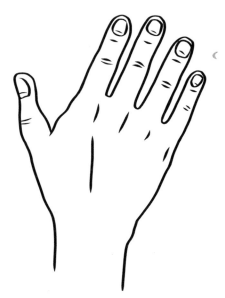

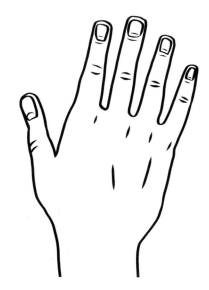

ELEMENTAL HAND

Qualities: Large palm; short, thick fingers with clear major lines on the palm.

They are: Faithful, industrious, predictable.

They need: Routine, security.

SQUARE HAND

Qualities: Largish fingers, medium-size square palm.

They are: Methodical, resilient, good organizers.

They need: Structure, order, to be part of a community.

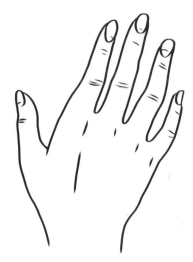

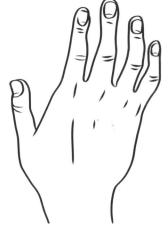

PSYCHIC HAND

Qualities: A small, well-balanced hand with pointed fingertips, smooth joints.

They are: Intuitive, spiritual, psychic, devoted, creative.

They need: A strong loving relationship.

SPATULATE OR ACTIVE HAND

Qualities: Broad, rounded fingertips, flattish fingers, often pronounced joints.

They are: Determined, optimistic, pioneering.

They need: Routine, security, order.

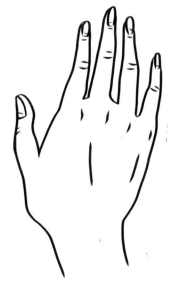

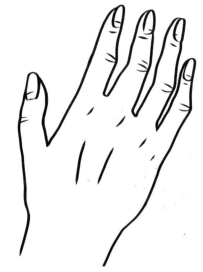

CONIC HAND

Qualities: Tapered fingertips and tapered palm.

They are: Sensitive, artistic, creative, highly visual.

They need: Sensual stimuli.

PHILOSOPHIC HAND

Qualities: Tapered fingertips, large and/or knotty joints, broad lower phalanges.

They are: Systematic, detail-oriented, reserved, knowledgeable.

They need: Absorbing work, kindred spirits.

MIXED HAND

Qualities: A combination of two of more of the above.

The Four Elemental Hand Shapes

If you have a mix of hand types, read the interpretations for both descriptions.

EARTH HAND

Qualities: Square palm; short fingers; clear, strong major lines on the palm.

They are: Fixers—reliable, pragmatic, direct.

They need: Routine, security, order.

AIR HAND

Qualities: Square palms; long fingers; clear, thin major lines on the palm.

They are: Communicators—talkative, analytical, cerebral.

They need: Emotional balance; ways to safely express feelings.

FIRE HAND

Qualities: Rectangular palms; short fingers; clear major and minor lines on the palm.

They are: Adventurers—energetic, sociable, passionate.

They need: To conserve energy by saying no on occasion, to release excess energy through exercise.

WATER HAND

Qualities: Rectangular palms; long fingers; thin major lines and lots of fine lines on the palm.

They are: Intuitives—emotional, sensitive, imaginative.

They need: Peace, time out, grounding through doing practical tasks.

JOINT FLEXIBILITY

Feel the flexibility of the whole hand and look at the thumb and finger joints. The interpretations below can modify your hand type. For example, if you have a Fire hand, which shows energy and ambition, but with knotty joints, this shows that you can slow down enough to pay attention to the finer detail—a great combination for success. If the hand feels generally stiff overall, and you fit the Air hand type, this can reveal single-mindedness or stubbornness.

▸ **Knotty or prominent joints:** Attention to detail, efficiency.

▸ **Smooth joints:** Intuitive approach, driven by instincts.

▸ **Stiffness of the hands:** Rigid, or committed, attitudes.

▸ **Flexible joints:** Versatility, openness.

However, hand flexibility can be affected due to age. Check the finger and phalanx lengths (see page 97 and 100) and the lines of the palm to build a whole picture.

THE FINGERTIPS

The tips of the fingers—the fingertip shape, nail shape, and fingerprint features—offer a wealth of meaning.

Fingertip shape: To determine your fingertip shape, look at their shape from the palm side, so you're not influenced by the shape of your fingernails. There are four basic types: pointed, conic, square, and spatulate.

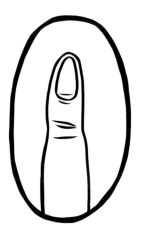

Pointed:
Sensitive, intuitive, imaginative.

Conic:
Impulsive, inconsistent.

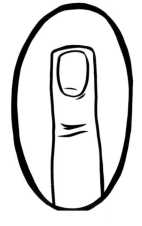

Square:
Practical, conventional.

Spatulate:
Entrepreneurial, motivated.

Nail shape and color: The nails suggest character attributes and can be an indicator of health—for example, bitten nails can indicate stress.

There are four basic nail shapes: short, long, narrow, and broad. To see if you have long or short nails, look just at the pink part of the nail, between the cuticle and white tip. If this is approximately half the length of the top phalange of that finger or thumb, the nail is considered average length. If the nail is more than half, it is considered long, and if it is less than half, it is considered short.

If the nails are wider than their length (with length meaning the pink part of the nail down to the cuticle), they are considered broad. To identify a narrow nail, you'll need to go by what you see: If there's a generous amount of flesh on each side of the nail, it is likely the nails are narrow.

Long: Gentle, calm, imaginative.

Short: Self-critical, analytical, insightful, can be stubborn.

Narrow: Sensitive; if very narrow, prone to anxiety.

Broad: Emotional, hot-tempered, optimistic.

FINGERTIP MARKINGS

To see the features on your fingertips, you may need to use a magnifying glass or take fingerprints (see Palm Prints on page 103). Often, people have a combination of the three major markings: arches, whorls, and loops. When you've identified which you have, note the fingers on which they appear, then use the finger meaning to give an interpretation. For example, a whorl on the index (Jupiter) finger combines the whorl meaning (individuality) with the Jupiter meaning of ambition, so this would indicate you have a unique talent or skill you use in your professional and/or creative life (see the meanings of the fingers and mounts on page 94).

Arches:
Practical and methodical; often clever with the hands. The need for security and routine. An arched fingerprint has a wave-like pattern.

Whorls:
Individuality; someone who has a special talent or skill. A whorl is a spiral with lines curling around it.

Loops:
Sociable, communicative; a connector. A loop has radiating lines.

THE **THREE ZONES** OF THE PALM

You can also look at the shape of the hand to see what motivates you most: ideas, intellect, and spirituality; practical achievements; or the material world of money, security, and sex. The whole hand can be divided into three zones, as follows:

Fingers: The mental and intuitive zone: intellect, spirituality, brain power.

Middle of palm, including outer and inner Mars: The practical zone: self-management, work-life balance, practical tasks.

Lower palm, including the thumb: The material zone: money, security, drives and instincts, sex.

See which part of the hand is most prominent. What is your first impression—are your fingers long, or maybe the lower side of your hand is large and fleshy? Proportionally large fingers show an emphasis on the mental world, so you may spend a lot of time in your head. If the lower palm is prominent, then you're driven more by material and instinctual needs, such as sex, money, and security.

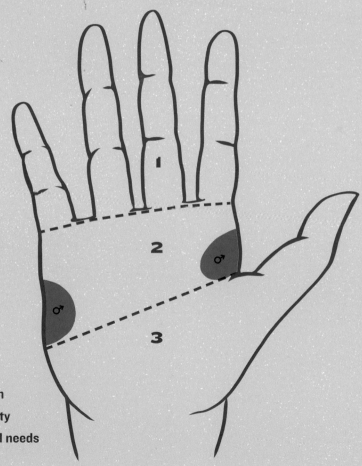

1 Intellect and intuition
2 Action and practicality
3 Instinct and physical needs

There are seven primary mounts and one plain on the hands. They are named after the seven classical planets. Read the mounts for instant insight into a person's character. When you start to read the lines on the palm, knowing the meaning of the mounts helps you effectively interpret them.

The names of the mounts under the fingers are also given to that finger, so, for example, the Mount of Apollo is under the index, or Apollo, finger. The planet Mars, for aggression and energy, appears three times—as the inner mount of Mars, the outer mount of Mars, and the plain of Mars in the center of the palm. We also have Venus, under the thumb, and the mount of the Moon, opposite the Venus mount.

Slightly cup the palm to see the mounts. You'll find that some are excessively developed, some are prominent and fleshy, some are flat, and some might merge with their neighbor. The higher, or more developed, the mount, the more of the qualities of that mount you have. Overall, the ideal palm has equally well-developed mounts. The mount interpretations, like the lengths of the fingers, are based on the associations of the planets linked with each mount.

Well-developed: Risen, but not excessively.

Overdeveloped: Overdeveloped, fleshy, prominent.

Flat: Flat, thin, unremarkable.

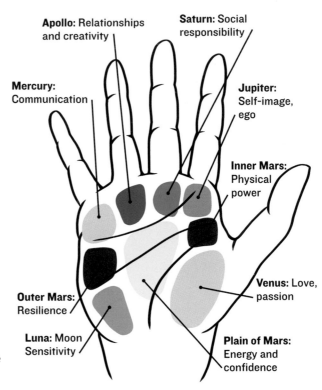

Apollo: Relationships and creativity

Saturn: Social responsibility

Mercury: Communication

Jupiter: Self-image, ego

Inner Mars: Physical power

Outer Mars: Resilience

Venus: Love, passion

Luna: Moon Sensitivity

Plain of Mars: Energy and confidence

You can combine finger-length readings (see page 97) with mount readings. For example, if you have a short index (Apollo) finger and a flat mount of Apollo beneath it, this could show great dips in self-confidence, as low self-confidence is reflected in both the short index finger and flat mount. If you have an average-length index finger and flat Apollo mount, this would give the meaning that you're mostly balanced in your outlook but can lack confidence at times. It's easy to remember as follows:

MERGED MOUNTS

Sometimes, a mount may appear flat, but it has merged with the mount next to it. Merged mounts have interpretations based on the two mounts:

Jupiter and Saturn merged: Competitive, enterprising, practical ambition.

Apollo and Saturn merged: Can put ideas into practice, creative and practical.

Mercury and Apollo merged: A career in writing and communication.

- A long finger above a mount increases the attributes of that mount.
- A short finger above a mount reduces the attributes of that mount.
- An average-length finger above a mount adds balance.

Take note of your palm's mounts and then look up the interpretations on the following pages. Also, look to the lines of the palm for more information (see page 104), as this can balance out flat mounts and show excessive qualities, too. For example, you might have doubts about a person with an overdeveloped mount of Mercury because they might exaggerate a little to please people, but if they have a well-defined head line, which shows trust, then you can rely upon them to tell the truth. If the mount of Jupiter is well developed, meaning a love of learning and an enterprising nature, look at the head line for confirmation. A well-marked head line supports this meaning, whereas a weak head line exaggerates the meaning and suggests egotism.

MOUNT OF MERCURY

Mercury Qualities: Self-expression, communicating ideas.

Well-developed: Natural connector, honesty, commercial acumen.

Overdeveloped: Keen to please, so may omit difficult truths. If the little (Mercury) finger is crooked, dishonesty and misinformation.

Flat: Poor communication skills, shyness.

MOUNT OF APOLLO

Apollo Qualities: Creativity, sociability, emotions, the subconscious.

Well-developed: Artistic tendencies, charismatic, optimistic, versatile.

Overdeveloped: Attention-seeking, insensitive.

Flat: Focused outlook, limited interests beyond everyday affairs.

MOUNT OF SATURN

It is rare to have a developed mount of Saturn; on many hands, it is not well defined, so as an alternative, read the interpretations for the Saturn finger (see page 101).

Saturn Qualities: Responsibility, morality, seriousness.

Well-developed: Conservative, practical, reliable, cautious, studious.

Overdeveloped: Philosophical, serious, can be the gloomy martyr.

Flat: Wants to be cared for, can shirk responsibility.

MOUNT OF JUPITER

Jupiter Qualities:
Ambition, success,
self-confidence, leadership,
pride, ego.

Well-developed:
Enterprising, focused,
loves to learn.

Overdeveloped:
Domineering, unreasonable, opinionated.

Flat: Can lack confidence, prefers direction
from others.

MOUNT OF MARS (INNER)

Inner Mars Qualities:
Physical power, self-esteem,
physical courage, energy.

Well-developed: Well
balanced and honest, will
take determined action if
necessary.

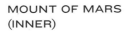

Overdeveloped: Aggressive, impulsive, could
show anger physically.

Flat: Low self-esteem, insecurity.

MOUNT OF MARS (OUTER)

Outer Mars Qualities:
Resilience, willpower, inner
strength, moral courage.

Well-developed: Good
self-control, takes appropriate action, loyal.

Overdeveloped: Impetuousness, irrationality,
pomposity.

Flat: Overly passive, avoids confrontation,
difficulty making commitments.

PLAIN OF MARS

Assess the plain of Mars by
touching it.

Plain of Mars Qualities:
Confidence, energy.

Deep and firm: Balanced,
secure, practical, confident. A
hard feel can show lack of tact.

Soft and fleshy: Lack of
motivation.

Soft and thin: A giver, can give too much energy
to others, may lack confidence.

MOUNT OF THE MOON

Moon Qualities: Sensitivity,
creativity, imagination,
intuition.

Well-developed: Artistic sense,
compassionate, intuitive,
receptive.

Overdeveloped: Imaginative,
fantastical, ungrounded.

Flat: Skepticism, tactlessness.

MOUNT OF VENUS

Venus Qualities: Love, emotion, passion, beauty, vitality.

Well-developed: Good relationships, happiness, energy.

Overdeveloped: High
libido, impetuousness,
pleasure-seeking.

Flat: Low sex drive, lack of
motivation, difficulty connecting with others.

INTERPRETING **FINGER LENGTHS**

To interpret finger lengths, examine the fingers in terms of their relative proportions. For example, your little finger is considered long if the tip extends beyond the upper joint of your ring finger (even if all your fingers appear small and short). When you've noted this, the interpretations for the fingers that follow will make much more sense; you'll be able to choose the interpretations that best reveal particular aspects of your life.

Look at your finger lengths from the palm side, rather than the back of your hand, and cup your palm to get the straightest line where the fingers join the palm. As most people's palms are curved, this allows you to see the relative finger lengths more accurately than looking at a flat palm. Try it: Stretch out your palm and look at the relative lengths of your fingers. Now, cup your palm so the bases of the fingers align, and the relative lengths will shift—particularly if you have a very curved palm.

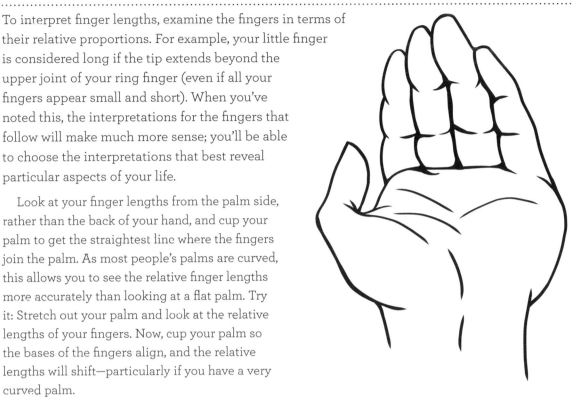

With your fingers together, cup your hand to make a straight line across the base of the fingers. Then, look at the relative finger lengths from this position. Determine if your relative finger lengths are average, long, or short according to these descriptions:

INDEX FINGER

Average: Stops halfway up the top phalange of the middle finger.

Short: Lower than the halfway point.

Long: Extends beyond the halfway point.

MIDDLE FINGER

Average: The finger is about the same length as the back of the hand (measuring from the knuckle to the wrist bone) or three-quarters of the length of the palm. Check this by placing the middle finger of one hand on the palm of the other hand, lining up the base of the finger with the base of the wrist.

Short: Less than the above.

Long: More than the above.

RING FINGER

Average: Stops halfway up the top phalange of the middle finger.

Short: Lower than the halfway point.

Long: Extends beyond the halfway point.

LITTLE FINGER

Average: Reaches the top joint of the ring finger.

Short: Lower than the top joint.

Long: Extends beyond the top joint.

THUMB

To see your relative thumb length, hold the thumb in against the side of the palm.

Average: Stops halfway up the base phalange of the index finger.

Short: Lower than the halfway point.

Long: Extends beyond the halfway point.

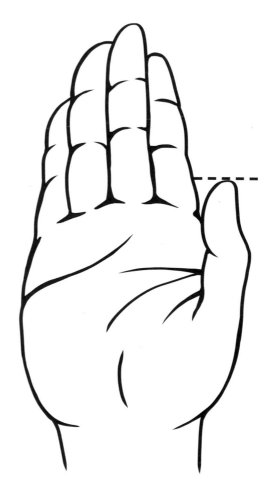

This thumb is considered short, as it stops before the halfway point on the index finger.

FINGER- AND THUMB-LENGTH MEANINGS

The fingers and thumb each link with an aspect of the self. Overall, the longer the finger or thumb, the stronger the attributes. Short fingers or thumbs diminish the attribute, as follows.

Average	Short	Long
Index finger: Ambition; leadership; self-confidence		
Well-balanced; realistic self-image	Lacking confidence	Strong; can be driven; if very long, intolerant
Middle finger: Resilience; morality; responsibility		
Good work-life balance	Uncertain; fears pressure	Overgiving; dependable
Ring finger: Creativity; emotions; the subconscious		
Articulate; sociable; open	Lower energy; cautious	Emotional; passionate; entrepreneurial
Little finger: Communication; communicating		
Balanced; good listener	Shy; difficulty	Charismatic; talkative; good with words; can be impetuous
Thumb: Ego and willpower		
Reasonable drive and assertiveness	Team player; may lack motivation	Natural leader; could be domineering

INTERPRETING **THE PHALANGES**

As with finger lengths, determining whether the phalanges are average, short, or long is relative, so you're comparing these areas of your fingers to each other. Hold up your hand and look at the relative lengths of the phalanges on each finger. Are they even, or is one shorter or longer?

A quick way to read your phalanges is via the division of the top, middle, and lower into three categories (these categories also correspond to the three zones of the palm). The length of a phalange reveals how you think and act: long top phalanges (1) show you operate intuitively and focus on thinking; longer middle phalanges (2) show you're concerned more with action and practical tasks; and longer lower phalanges (3) denote that you're more concerned with the material world: money, security, and physical needs.

The fleshiness of a phalange also reveals an emphasis on these three categories. If your base phalanges, for example, are long and fleshy, this shows that having money and holding on to it is a key priority for you.

The thumb represents strength of character, and it's divided into two phalanges. The top phalange rules willpower and ability, while the lower phalange rules logic and reason. Look at the proportion of the phalanges—are they equal in length? Is one phalange fleshier than the other? If the top phalange is dominant in length and shape, this may show that your ambition sometimes overrides practicalities. If the lower phalange is larger or longer than the top phalange, you put practical considerations first

rather than let ambition rule. The thumb is also an indicator of temper. A bulbous and/or red top phalange can show a fiery nature. If the thumb is broad and square at the tip and the top of the thumb is fleshy and rounded, this denotes anger and passion, but also insensitivity.

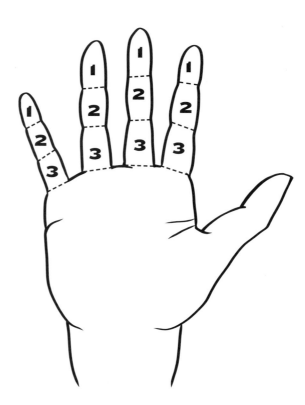

1 **Intellect and intuition**

2 **Action and practicality**

3 **Instinct and physical needs**

Hold the back of your hand to the light or a light background, resting your elbow on a surface so you can see the natural position of your fingers. You may see that some fingers have prominent gaps between them, or they might naturally lean closer to other fingers.

For example, is there a pronounced gap between your little finger and ring finger? Or maybe your index finger naturally leans toward your middle finger. Whatever your natural finger positions, gaps and leaning fingers have individual interpretations. These meanings are based upon planets associated with the mounts of the hand and the fingers:

• The index finger is ruled by Jupiter, the planet of self-confidence, pride, and ego.

• The middle finger is ruled by Saturn, the planet of responsibility, authority, and conscientiousness.

• The ring finger is ruled by Apollo, the planet of creativity and the emotions.

• The little finger is ruled by Mercury, the planet of communication and honesty.

So, for example, the meaning of a gap between the index and middle finger denotes good separation between the attributes of these two planets; the person can separate, or balance, personal ego with responsibility to others. When the index finger leans toward the middle finger, this is interpreted as the index finger tending to, or needing, the qualities of the middle finger; a person's self-confidence depends upon having security and being conscientious in their work, for example. When the middle finger leans toward the ring finger, we have the combination of responsibility (Saturn) with emotion and relationships, suggesting family commitments.

INDEX FINGER

Gap between index finger and middle finger: Good time management.

Index finger leans toward middle finger: Needs security, money is important, cautious.

MIDDLE FINGER

Gap between the middle finger and index finger: Good time management.

Gap between the middle finger and ring finger: Spontaneity, lives for the day, not a planner, can be erratic with money.

Middle finger leans toward the index finger: Needs more confidence.

Middle finger leans toward the ring finger: Family commitments, lots of responsibility, would like to take life less seriously.

RING FINGER

Gap between the ring finger and the middle finger: Spontaneity, lives for the day, not a planner, can be erratic with money.

Gap between the ring finger and the little finger: Someone who's a bit distanced from the rest of the world.

Ring finger leans toward middle finger: Someone who wants to be more responsible.

Ring finger leans toward little finger: Flair for words.

LITTLE FINGER

Gap between little finger and ring finger: A dreamer, prefers the spiritual to the material world.

Little finger leans toward ring finger: Prone to exaggeration, emotionally driven.

Crooked little finger: Someone who is not straight with the facts, who embroiders the truth or lies.

DOES MONEY RUN THROUGH YOUR FINGERS?

Put your fingers together and hold up your hand to the light or to a light background. If you see gaps between your fingers at their base (the base phalanges), this shows openness, sharing, generosity, and friendliness. If the gaps are wide, it can show that you find it hard to hold on to money—it flows through your fingers. If there are no gaps between the base phalanges and they appear thick and fleshy, you like the finer things in life and material possessions—including holding on to money—are a priority.

CHIROMANCY

The palm has four major lines and numerous minor lines and markings. Taken with what we know about the hand's shape, we can now build a bigger picture of a person's life. The skill here is to combine chirognomy—reading the shape of the hand, fingers, and thumbs—with chiromancy, the interpretation of the markings and lines on the palm.

PALM PRINTS

Making a palm print is the best way to clearly see the major and minor lines of the hand. You'll need watercolor paint, which washes off easily after use, a small paint roller, paper, and a flat surface. Take prints of both the right and left hands by applying paint to the palm and fingers and pressing onto the paper, making sure there are no paint blobs on the roller. Then, date your prints. As the palm lines can change over time, the prints give you a record for future reference.

MAJOR LINES

The four major lines are the life line, head line, heart line, and fate line. They denote life events, how you think, your relationships, and your career path. As with chirognomy, remember to refer to the left hand as well as the right during a reading, so you can see how a person has developed (or has not been aware of) certain talents and abilities.

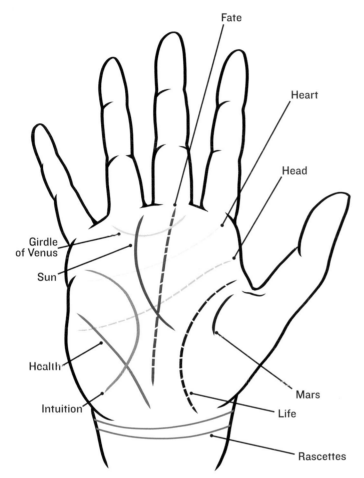

Fate

Heart

Head

Girdle of Venus

Sun

Health

Intuition

Mars

Life

Rascettes

The Life Line: Health and Vitality

The life line on the left hand: Inherited traits.

The life line on the right hand: How you have dealt with inherited traits.

Description and location: This is the line that encircles the thumb. It begins above the thumb and ends toward the base of the palm.

Length of the life line: The length of the line doesn't denote how many years you will live. It divides into five-year periods, so to see timings, work with the length of the life line you have. Most palmistry diagrams show seventy-five years as an average.

How it is marked: A clearly marked life line means strength, energy, and good health. A stronger life line on the left hand shows living more according to destiny; if the line is stronger on the right hand, this indicates greater self-confidence. A weaker life line means less energy and more susceptibility to illness (see also "The Health Line," page 110, which can suggest a stronger or weaker constitution).

A life line made up of lots of short, unconnected lines can show oversensitivity and nervousness, but also potential artistic brilliance. Noticeable gaps in the life line, such as islands, chains, and other markings (see page 114), can show illnesses, stress, or other disruptions. Rays, or horizontal lines, coming from the mount of Venus across the life line represent troubles and challenges.

OTHER FEATURES:

Guardian angel lines: These lines begin on the life line and extend downward. It's believed that they represent people lost at a specific age (see the illustration on page 109 to date your guardian angel lines). When someone close to you dies, they are thought to become guardian angels in your life, so you may see these lines representing,

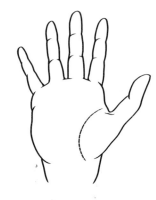

for example, relatives or close friends.

Rising lines: If there are lines rising from the life line, see where they end, as this shows your efforts to achieve success in a particular area. For example, a rising line that finishes on the mount of Saturn, below the middle finger, shows a striving toward greater social responsibility.

Double life line: This is a fainter line that runs alongside the life line and shows protection from life's difficulties. Some palmists also read the double line as a sign of prosperity and happiness.

The curve of the life line: The bigger the curve, the more generous the person is and the more energy they have for other people. A slight curve or virtually straight life line running across the mount of Venus suggests a focus on the self.

The angle of the life line and head line: Cup your hand a little to see if the life line touches the head line. If it touches, this means prosperity. If the lines do not touch, look at the angle they make. The sharper the angle, the greater the luck.

Look on both hands for this: Some people have a life and head line that are apart on their left hand but have a touching life and head line on their right hand, showing that they have taken their destiny into their own hands, perhaps maximizing opportunities for wealth or becoming otherwise connected to it, such as through family or a partner.

You can also look at the point at which the head line and life line separate, as this reveals the age at which you gained independence as an adult (see "Timing," page 109).

The Head Line: How You Think

The head line on the left hand: The intelligence you were born with.

The head line on the right hand: How you have developed your thinking.

Description and location: This is a horizontal line beginning on the thumb side of the palm that is above, crossing, or touching the life line. Note where the head line begins and where it ends, as these locations have meanings.

Length of the head line: A long head line can be a sign of high intelligence and a philosophical outlook; however, this person may use this ability to further their interests rather than directly helping others. A short head line shows a focus more on practical, immediate issues and could show that you are focused on a particular life area. Look on the palm to see where the head line begins and ends, as it has one of the following meanings:

Beginning on the mount of Jupiter, under the index finger: Confidence and ambition.

Beginning below the life line, so it crosses the life line: Lack of confidence, risk-averse.

Ending toward or on the mount of the Moon: Imagination and mysticism, artistic ability.

Ending toward or on the mount of Mercury, below the little finger: Business or scientific leanings.

Ending toward or on the mount of Saturn, under the middle finger: Belief, philosophical thought, music.

How it is marked: A strong, unbroken head line reveals good concentration, whereas a fainter line can show a lack of focus and possibly poor concentration. A broken head line may also be an indicator of headaches. Chains and breaks can mean obstacles and career challenges.

OTHER FEATURES:

The writer's fork: A fork at the end of the head line on the mount of the Moon is known as the writer's fork because it denotes creativity in writing; it's a sign of literary talent.

A branch line from the head line to the heart line: This denotes a love or fascination that may become obsessive. The heart rules the head—more so if a strong heart line lies close to the headline.

The angle of the head line and life line: See "The Angle of the Life Line and Head Line" on page 104.

THE SIMIAN LINE

A simian line is rare. It's a single line that appears on the palm, replacing the head and heart lines. This means that thought and emotion are as one, so a person with a simian line may struggle to separate emotional responses from logical reasoning. A simian line can show someone who is extremely focused, driven, and dedicated to a cause—but they may have obsessive tendencies, too.

The curve of the head line: A straight head line shows a logical approach to life and that material things are important—less so the imagination. A downward-curving head line, ending on or near the mount of the Moon, reveals an intuitive disposition, and the greater the slope, the more intuitive and imaginative that person will be. A head line that is generally straight but curves upward toward the side of the palm on the upper mount of Mars shows business success—although this person could also be an unreasonable, demanding boss. A line that begins straight then curves downward shows a mix between the logical and the intuitive—a person who has the balance right.

The Heart Line: Emotions and Relationships

Also known as: The mensal line or love line.

The heart line on the left hand: Your potential to love and to sustain relationships.

The heart line on the right hand: How you have developed that potential.

Description and location: This is a horizontal line running across the palm, above the head line (see page 105). The heart line begins around the outer edge of the palm. Note that some palmists read this line the other way around; however, in this book, we take the starting point of the line at the palm edge, under the mount of Mercury (at the base of the little finger), as this is where the line is usually strongest.

Length of the heart line: A long line, extending right across the palm to the inner edge, shows a person who experiences strong or excessive emotions but can be so driven by their feelings that they entertain unreasonable jealousy and possessiveness. Shorter heart lines usually end on one of the following locations on the palm:

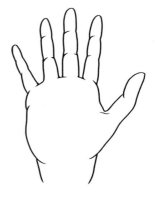

Under the mount of Jupiter, under the index finger: This person is loyal and a romantic at heart but tends to idealize partners. For some palmists, this type of line-ending means fame to come.

Between the middle and index fingers: A sign of a realist—loving, but down to earth.

The mount of Saturn, under the middle finger: This is a passionate person who can be overly serious.

How it is marked: A strong heart line shows emotional security and stable relationships; a weak heart line shows emotional insecurity. Gaps in the heart line, lines of stress crossing it, and chains and islands can reveal relationship break-ups and other emotional issues.

OTHER FEATURES:

A forked heart line: When the heart line forks, with one line on the mount of Jupiter under the index finger and the other line between the index and middle fingers, this reveals happiness and affection in relationships.

The gap between the heart line and the head line: The wider the gap, the greater the person's openness and generosity. So, a narrow gap between the head line and heart line reveals a person who is more concerned with themselves than others. Another way of interpreting this narrow gap is to see which line is stronger. The stronger line means dominance, so a strong heart line close to the head line means the heart rules the head.

The curve of the heart line: A curved heart line shows strong physical desire—and someone who tends to initiate sex. A straight heart line can show a person who is happy not to be the initiator; this person may also be romantic but is less sexually driven. If the heart line curves downward and crosses the head line and life line, it's believed to be a sign of past emotional trauma.

The Fate Line: Career and Life Path

Also known as: The line of destiny, line of fortune, line of Saturn.

The fate line on the left hand: Your career potential.

The fate line on the right hand: How you have developed that potential.

Description and location: This is a vertical line that starts toward the bottom of the hand and extends upward toward the middle, or Saturn, finger.

Length of the fate line: A long line, extending from the rascettes on the wrist (see page 107) or mount of the Moon to beyond the heart line shows personal drive and need to achieve; this person may have a creative vocation that stays with them for life. Look on the palm to see where the fate line begins and ends, as it shows at what life stage you have experienced, or can expect to achieve, success—and the kind of success that's available to you.

Beginning at the life line: If strong, shows deserved success and merit. If low down on the life line, shows that early life may have been heavily influenced by the wishes of parents or other caregivers.

Beginning at the wrist, extends straight up to the mount of Saturn, under the middle finger: Great success.

Beginning on the mount of the Moon: Success that is dependent on your reputation.

Beginning on the head line and strongly marked: Success comes later in life through hard work and talent.

Beginning high in the plain of Mars (usually between the head line and heart line): Difficulties—but if the line is strong afterward, shows difficulties overcome; the second half of life is often better than the first.

Beginning on the heart line: Success late in life after a difficult struggle.

Ending on the mount of Jupiter, under the index finger: Success and power. If the fate line has a branch going onto this mount, it shows early career success.

Ending on the mount of Apollo: Success in the arts.

Ending on the mount of Saturn: See the interpretation for the long fate line on page 107.

Ending on the mount of Mercury: Success in business and communications.

Ending at the head line: A mistake halts success; alternatively, this person may be dedicated to a profession until they are around forty, then choose another path (forty is the approximate age at which the fate line hits the head line).

Ending at the heart line: Love gets in the way of success, or a person changes his direction to do something he loves, whether this is work-related or not; this is often shown by a new branch of the fate line rising from the heart line.

How it is marked: A strong, unbroken fate line shows a clear life and career direction, and that you feel in control of events and your life direction. A fainter line shows uncertainty in your career, and breaks literally show career breaks. If you see a fork, it shows having more than one interest or career; if there are little prongs with the fork, these show the number of new interests that call. If the forks develop into marked branches, see the areas of the palm where these branches end, as they show the life area that will capture this person's interest; the interpretations for these are as for the ending points listed previously. For example, a branch running to the mount of Jupiter shows success early in that person's career.

OTHER FEATURES: A double or sister line next to the fate line shows two careers that you will follow.

CHILDHOOD INFLUENCES

You can look at childhood happiness and relationships by examining the beginnings of the major lines. Do these lines start strong, and are they well marked? This reveals emotional stability and happiness, whereas interruptions on the line or faint, broken lines can show difficulties and instability in childhood years. Look at the lines on the left hand, as this hand shows us what that person inherited—their given circumstances—while the right hand shows the effect of their circumstances and if they created change and manifested different outcomes.

TIMING AND THE MAJOR LINES

The four major lines—the life line, heart line, head line, and fate line—are divided into years. The timing begins where the lines begin on the hand, so remember to read the lines from their starting points. An average life span of seventy-five years is used, but you will need to revise this if you are reading for a person older than seventy-five.

To begin, you may like to see how your line timings relate to events in the past and then look beyond your current age to see what may potentially happen in the future. As you have free will, these show likely events based on current circumstances.

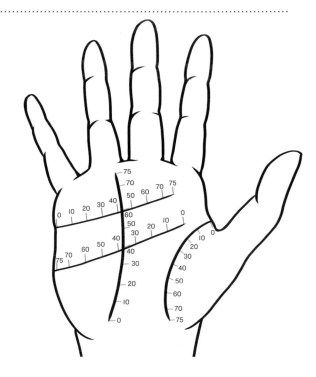

THE MINOR LINES

The minor lines include the Sun line, girdle of Venus, line of intuition, health line, marriage lines, line of Mars, children lines, and rascettes. You may have none or some of these lines, and some may be faint. If any lines are faint or absent, it does not have a negative connotation— in fact, a missing health line, for example, is seen as a positive sign (see page 110). Consider the minor lines as a source of additional or supporting evidence, adding it to what you have already gleaned from examining the hand and the major lines.

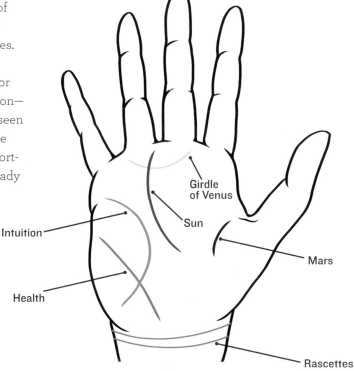

Sun Line: Success, Prosperity, and Creativity

Also known as: The Apollo line, line of brilliance, line of success.

If absent, this is not a bad sign; look at the fate line for clues as to a person's success. If present, it enhances the positive attributes of the fate line (see page 106).

Description and location: A vertical line ending on the mount of Apollo (under the ring finger), it begins on or just above the wrist, on the mount of the Moon, or higher up on the hand. If you cannot find it, look first for a vertical line on the mount of Apollo and follow it downward.

Length of the Sun line: Generally, the longer the line and the lower on the palm it begins, the greater the success potential. However, if it begins higher on the hand and is strongly defined, it can show prosperity later in life, after the person has found the right career path. The point at which the line begins is also associated with the following qualities and outcomes:

Beginning on the mount of the Moon: Conditions that support success; success that comes from influential contacts.

Beginning on or near the life line: Appreciation of the arts and love of beauty. If other signs on the hand are artistic—such as the writer's fork at the end of the head line (see page 105)—this reveals practical achievement in the arts.

Beginning on or near the head line: The willpower to succeed.

Beginning on or near the heart line: Following a goal close to your heart; passionate motivation.

Beginning on or near the fate line: Great achievements.

Other features: A star on this line shows amazing success.

Health Line: General Health and Stress

Also known as: The Mercury, hepatic, or liver line.

If absent, this is a positive sign, generally meaning good health. If present, it can show whether someone is more resilient or vulnerable to stress and illness. A strong health line is more favorable than a weak line (see below).

Description and location: The line begins at the base of the palm, running almost diagonally over the palm to end below the mount of Mercury, under the little finger.

How it is marked: A strong health line indicates resilience to illness and stress and the ability to manage energy levels well. A faint line with breaks can show a weak constitution, a tendency to worry about potential health issues,

and potential illnesses. If there is a significant gap in the line, however, this is believed to show freedom from health problems during the gap period—you can time this from the illustration on page 109.

It is advisable to look at the life line, which also indicates health, when reading the health line (see page 104). Also, bear in mind that it is not appropriate to try to diagnose or predict health problems during a reading.

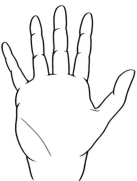

Line of Intuition: Clairvoyance

Also known as: The psychic line, line of inspiration, bow of intuitions.

If present, the line shows psychic ability and strong intuition. If absent, you or the person you are reading for may still have psychic leanings—look for a long, pointed ring finger, a head line sloping downward onto the mount of the Moon, or the mystic cross marking (see page 114).

Description and location: This is a usually faint line forming a curve from the mount of the Moon to the mount of Mercury, under the little finger.

How it is marked: Even if faint, the presence of this line is still significant. It is believed that the stronger the line, the greater the psychic ability a person has. Examine the left hand to see if the line of intuition is present; if it is, you or the person you are reading for was born with this attribute. The right hand shows if this ability is being used.

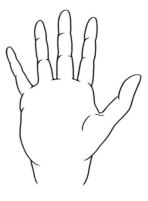

Line of Mars: Extra Strength and Passion

If present, the line of Mars denotes physical strength and strong drives. If absent, it does not mean you lack vitality and passion; you may have a line of Mars on your left hand or a strong life line (see page 104), which, if present, also indicates these qualities.

Description and location: This is a curved line within the life line on the mount of Venus. It is not to be confused with the double life line (see page 104), which runs close to the life line.

How it is marked: The stronger the line, the more powerful a person's strength and passion. The Mars line should also be interpreted with the life line because it moderates or enhances its properties. If the life line is weak, with breaks showing potential illness or low energy, the line of Mars brings energy, so the outlook for that person would be more positive. If a Mars line appears with a strong life line, this can indicate intense passion and energy. According to Cheiro, on a hand that is broad or square, such as an elementary or square hand, a line of Mars shows a person with a fighting temperament.

There is also a saying that if the line of Mars begins on the life line, this gives the age at which a love affair began or will begin.

Girdle of Venus: Passion and Sensitivity

If present, this line denotes sensuality and passion, which may be expressed in relationships, a personal belief, or a dedicated cause. If absent, it does not mean that the person lacks passion or emotion; look at the mount of Venus and heart line (see page 106), for example, for an indication of emotions and sex drive.

Description and location: This is a broken or unbroken semicircle that runs between the index and middle finger and the ring finger and little finger, over the mounts of Apollo and Saturn. The line can also extend to the edge of the palm, joining up with the marriage line (see page 113).

How it is marked: A faint girdle of Venus is considered better than a strong, unbroken marking, which indicates intense passion and emotion that may get in the way of decision making. A broken girdle is actually more positive, as it shows more emotional balance.

Length of the girdle of Venus: The girdle will usually end between the ring and little fingers but can end on the side of the palm, as below:

Ending on the edge of the palm, joined to the marriage line: Very exacting standards in relationships.

As above, but with breaks in the line: High expectations in love, but not unreasonably so.

Rascettes: Health and Travel

Also known as: Bracelets of Neptune.

Description and location: This can be one, two, or three lines running across the wrist. They are traditionally believed to be indicators of health.

How they are marked: Bend your wrist slightly to see how the lines are marked. If clearly marked, they show good health. Two lines are considered ideal. But do refer primarily to the life line (page 104) and health line (page 110) if present, for health indicators. If the first line arches up onto the palm, this can be interpreted, in a woman's hand, as fertility problems. If the first line is chained or broken, this suggests a weak constitution and a need to take extra care of your health. If the lines below it are strong, this gives a more positive health interpretation.

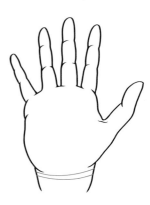

Other features: Vertical lines running up from the rascettes to the mount of the Moon show the urge to travel.

Some palmists believe that rascettes are signs of good luck, so three rascettes would signify excellent fortune.

Marriage Lines: Significant Relationships

Also known as: Relationship lines, lines of affection.

If present, these lines show significant love relationships, including marriage; there is one line for each relationship. If absent, you or the person you are reading for may have had relationships, but none yet of great significance. Look at the left hand to see if a marriage line, or lines, are present, as this shows the potential for these relationships in the future.

Description and location: These are horizontal

lines beginning on the side of the palm and extending to the mount of Mercury under the little finger (cupping the hand shows these lines, if present, more clearly).

How they are marked: The longer and deeper the line, the deeper the attachment.

Children Lines

When present, these lines show the number of children you have or will potentially have. This includes stepchildren, adopted children, and other children you have a strong bond with. Present on a male hand, children lines show the man is fond of children; the number of children is believed to be shown on a female hand. If children lines are absent on a male or female hand, this can show that a man or woman may not want to have children or is not ready. Check the mount of Venus: If it's flat, there is less inclination to have children; if it's fleshy, more so. A fleshy mount of Venus is also an indicator of fertility. Also, see if there is a branch line running from the heart line up to the mount of Saturn, under the middle finger, as this can also indicate the desire for children.

Description and location: These are vertical lines that rise from marriage lines or appear close to them.

How they are marked: Children lines are believed to be more deeply marked on a woman's hand than on a man's. Thick lines are believed to indicate boys, while thin lines show girls. A forked line shows twins. To count the number of children, count the lines from the outside of the palm.

TIMING YOUR RELATIONSHIPS

You can use the marriage or relationship line(s) on your hand to see the ages at which you committed, or will commit, to relationships. Imagine that the area between the top of the heart line and the start of the little finger is divided into three sectors. Each one represents twenty-five years. The halfway point is thirty-seven years. So, if you have a marriage line about halfway, this would show a major commitment at around the age of thirty-seven.

The Great Triangle: Health and Good Fortune

Description and location: The great triangle is an indicator of health and good fortune. It is formed by the intersections of the life line, head line, and health line.

How it is marked: A large, well-marked triangle is a sign of good physical health, strong character, and luck.

Mystic Cross: Esoteric Adventures

Description and location: This is a cross in the center of the palm, between the heart and head lines and the fate and Sun lines. (If you don't have a Sun line, look for a cross, either upright or diagonal, in the center of your palm between the heart and head lines.) This cross means interest in the occult.

Other Markings

See where these marks are located on the palm and relate them to the life area of the line or mount (see the illustration on page 104).

TRIANGLE: TALENT

Only read triangles that are well marked with strong lines. Triangles are considered good symbols because they mean talent and skill. If they appear on the mounts, they have the following meanings:

On the mount of Jupiter: Diplomacy.

On the mount of Saturn: Esoteric knowledge and clairvoyance.

On the mount of Apollo: Artistic ability.

On the mount of Mercury: Business acumen.

On the mount of upper Mars: Courage, martial strategy.

On the mount of lower Mars: Talent in science.

On the mount of the Moon: Ability to express imagination; travel.

On the mount of Venus: Great love.

STAR: SHOCKS

Five or more legs make a star; four would mean a cross (see below). Stars show shock events—for example, on the heart line it would indicate a relationship breakup or revelation that leads to a fundamental change in the nature of that relationship. One exception is a star on the mount of Jupiter, under the index finger, which denotes a particular success in your personal ambitions.

CROSS: DIFFICULTIES

A cross is generally a negative sign, meaning stress, disappointment, or difficulties. The exception to this rule:

On the mount of Jupiter: Because Jupiter stands for ego and ambition, the cross indicates a break in this attitude, denoting love and affection.

SQUARE: PROTECTION

A square is a sign of protection. It might surround a line or broken line or appear on a mount. It offsets any negatives in a line; time the appearance of the square, and you will see the time period of protection.

GRILLE: INTERFERENCE

Grilles, grids of crossed lines, denote problems and obstacles. An exception is, if the grille is on the mount of the Moon, and the Sun line is clearly marked, then the interpretation is literary talent, such as writing poetry or lyrics.

ISLANDS AND CHAINS: CONFUSION AND LOW ENERGY

Islands, when the line breaks into a small loop or other shape, are seen as negative because the energy of the line is weakened. Islands can mean confusion, doubt, and low energy. Chains are islands repeated on a line, which you interpret according to their location. For example, chaining on the life line might suggest a period of low energy and illness, which may also show up elsewhere on the palm.

CROSSBARS: LITTLE STOPPAGES

These small lines that cross a major or minor line mean an obstacle in the life area associated with that line. To check for crossbars on the fate line, for example, you would look for small horizontal lines placed across it; as the fate line reveals your career path, crossbars here would pinpoint a time of stress as your career path is blocked. As the line usually continues after the crossbar, this block is temporary. See the timing information (page 109) to work out at what age a block has, or might, occur.

5 FORTUNE-TELLING WITH CARDS

PLAYING CARDS AND TAROT

Cards have been telling our fortunes for hundreds of years. When we lay them out for a reading, we are presented with a visual representation of our situation; we can see where we are and where present influences might take us. With this knowledge, we are better positioned to meet challenges, make decisions, and more deeply understand ourselves. The cards' imagery, whether simple or complex, connects us with our inner knowing.

FORTUNE-TELLING WITH PLAYING CARDS

The genius of playing-card divination is in the cards' direct meanings and the specific interpretations that come from combinations of cards. There are no esoteric, layered meanings to remember. Learn the basics of each suit, and you will master the art of fortune-telling with playing cards.

During medieval times, playing cards, depending on their quality and design, were either commemorative (often enhanced with gold, like early Italian tarot cards) or used for gaming or educational purposes; theme decks of cards taught subjects ranging from flower names to geography. By the nineteenth century, fortune-telling with cards became popular due to the occult revival. However, in terms of bringing cartomancy to the everyday world, we owe a debt to Marie Anne Lenormand, the famous Parisian fortune-teller who divined with playing cards; she is credited with reading for Josephine, wife of Napoleon I, the French emperor.

The popularity of divining with cards continues today. The beauty of playing cards is that they have been, and can be, used by virtually everyone, from Roma travelers to heads of state.

A NOTE ON REVERSED CARDS

You can read reversed cards if you choose; reversed meanings for each card are given, but some readers prefer to give their own interpretations for reversals or ignore them altogether. Reversed meanings are not always negative; for example, reversed cards in duplicate numbers, such as four Nines, give you the timescale for an event, while reversals in four Tens reveal the number of obstacles you might encounter; identifying and understanding these can help you consider possible solutions.

SHUFFLING AND CHOOSING THE CARDS

Shuffle the cards, thinking of your question. You'll need to cut the deck, but the number of times you cut it depends on the layout you have chosen, so simply follow the guidance given for each layout.

If you're reading for another person, ask her to shuffle the cards and cut the deck according to the chosen layout, but you gather up the cards and lay them out, ready for the reading.

HOW TO BEGIN

You will need a standard deck of playing cards and a clean table or other surface on which to lay your cards. It's advisable to purchase a new deck that you use only for divination. Wrap them in dark fabric when they are not being used to protect their energies. Cards absorb our intentions; if you use an existing deck, the cards will have been programmed, through repeated use, for games—and divination work requires a different quality of attention.

Attune your new deck by touching all the cards to imprint them with your energy. Next, shuffle them and then hold them still. Close your eyes and set an intention that this is your divination deck and ask that all your readings with it are for the highest good. Spend a few minutes consciously making this connection with your cards.

Do not allow anyone else to handle your cards casually. When your deck is not in use, store it in a bag or box.

Before reading with your playing cards, you'll need to do two things:

1 Reduce the traditional fifty-two-card deck to thirty-two. Take out the twos, threes, fours, fives, and sixes from each suit and put them aside. The remaining thirty-two are your divination cards: the Aces, Sevens, Eights, Nines, Tens, Jacks, Queens, and Kings. (Keep the extra cards with the deck in case you want to try the thirty-six-card method on page 126.)

2 Make a mark at the top right-hand corner of each card to denote upright. This might be a cross or an asterisk, for example. Because reversed cards have a different meaning, you need to know if you're looking at an upright or reversed card in a reading (some cards naturally get reversed during shuffling). Up until the mid-nineteenth century, all playing cards had a single image, rather than the mirror-image cards of today: The suit symbols pointed in one direction and the Court cards (Kings, Queens, and Jacks) had feet, so our ancestors didn't need to mark their cards—but we do.

FORMULATING YOUR QUESTION

Consider your question as you shuffle the cards. Your question can be specific or a general request to know more about a certain life area. It is helpful to take a few calming breaths before you shuffle, allowing your mind to settle, so you are asking your question from a place of peace rather than anxiety or urgency.

THE ESSENTIAL LAYOUTS

There are many advanced techniques and layouts that can take time to master—and can be off-putting if this is your first foray into playing-card reading. Thus, these layouts are some of the simplest.

The Four Aces Method

In this layout, the answer or insight you need is quickly given based on how soon the four Aces appear when laying three rows of cards.

First, shuffle and choose your cards, laying down thirteen in a row. Then repeat, shuffling the remaining deck and dealing out another row of thirteen cards.

We interpret the cards in two stages:

1 Look at the position of the Aces across the rows. How many Aces appear and in what position? The higher the number of Aces, and the earlier they appear, the quicker you get what you hope for—and the more positive the result. The suits of the Aces tell you how easily and how soon your goal will be achieved and if you will encounter any obstacles. We divine this from the position of the Ace of Hearts because this card means "wish or goal achieved," so the interpretation stops with this card. Here's an example:

The two Aces in row 1 and two Aces in row 2 show that the outcome is favorable. All the Aces have turned up, and two appear in the first row. (If no Aces appeared in your first row and just one Ace in your second, for example, the interpretation would be unfavorable. So if you asked, "Will I hear from *x* person soon?" or "Will my examination/talk/game go well?" this gives a strong yes.

2 Next, we see that the Ace of Hearts is the second Ace in the reading. Again, the position of the Ace of Hearts is key because this represents success or the fulfillment of your wish. If the Ace of Hearts appears first, then you will get your wish soon, and you don't need to interpret the other Aces by their suit. If the Ace of Hearts appears last, you need to interpret all the preceding Aces.

In the example shown, the Ace of Spades appears first in the first row, followed by the Ace of Hearts. Putting the number of Aces in the reading (all four) together with the order in which they appear, we could say: Yes, you'll achieve your wish or get the result you hope for (four Aces), but the Ace of Spades says you will need to put in effort (so don't stop revising, practicing, or otherwise taking action toward your goal). If you do this now, you'll quickly succeed.

Here's a further example. If you got the Ace of Spades, then the Ace of Diamonds, the Ace of Clubs, and the Ace of Hearts, this advises you to work hard (Ace of Spades); be aware that you're being observed, so avoid sharing your ideas due to rivalry or jealousy (Ace of Diamonds); and reach out to friends or colleagues (Ace of Clubs). If you follow this advice, you'll receive your wish (Ace of Hearts). In summary:

Spades: Hard work, diligence and resilience.
Diamonds: Competition, rivalry, jealousy.
Clubs: Receiving help from others.
Hearts: You'll easily succeed.

| 1 | 2 | 3 | 4 | ACE ♠ | 6 | 7 | 8 | 9 | 10 | ACE ♥ | 12 | 13 |

| 1 | ACE ♦ | 3 | 4 | 5 | 6 | 7 | ACE ♣ | 9 | 10 | 11 | 12 | 13 |

Past, Present, Future: A Quick Reading

This three-card layout, or spread of cards, reveals three key issues or events. If you're reading for yourself, the cards will tell you what to pay attention to right now. The cards offer a flash of insight into your situation or your client's (so if your client does not wish to tell you why they have come for a reading, the cards will tell you). For more detail, you can progress to thirteen cards (see page 125).

There are two methods for selecting the three cards you'll need for this reading.

Method one: Shuffle your deck, thinking of your question or asking, "What do I need to know now?" and place it on a table, facedown. Cut it twice, using your left hand, so you have three piles of cards. Turn each pile over side to side, so you're looking at the card that was on the bottom of each pile. (You turn the piles over sideways to preserve the cards' upright or reversed position because upright and reversed cards have different meanings.)

Method two: Shuffle the cards and deal seven from the top of the pile, laying them in a row from left to right. Select the first, fourth, and seventh cards and discard the remaining ones.

You can interpret your three chosen cards as past, present, and future, or as aspects of your current situation.

Past, present, future: For a past, present, future reading, the card to the left is the past, the center card is the present, and the card to the right is future influences and possibilities.

Three aspects of now: To read the cards as three aspects of your current situation, look at their values. The card with the highest value (taking Ace as high) reveals the most important aspect now. For example, if you had the Seven of Hearts, Ace of Diamonds, and King of Clubs, you would take the Ace as the key focus. The Ace of Diamonds means an important document or letter. A basic interpretation would be the news or information you receive is about love or from someone who loves you (Seven of Hearts); the King of Clubs—a supportive, dark-haired man—may be that person. As the reading is about the present, rather than the future, it is likely that you will already know this individual.

Variation: You can allocate the meanings of three cards any way you wish. And if you prefer, you can choose three cards at random from the deck, facedown, rather than cards 1, 4, and 7.

EXAMPLE:

1: First card: Past

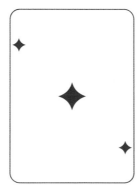

2: Fourth card: Present

3: Seventh card: Future

Past, Present, Future: Advanced Reading

For further insight into the past, present, and future, you can read with all thirty-two cards in the reduced deck. With this method, you end up with ten cards for each category, plus two Surprise cards. Surprise cards reveal unexpected events.

Shuffle the cards, thinking of your question, and divide them into two piles, facedown. Take the top card from each pile and place them to one side, facedown. These are the Surprise cards to be read later. Then, regather the rest of the

deck, shuffle once more, and deal them out into three piles with ten cards in each pile. The pile on the left represents the past; the center pile represents the present; and the right-hand pile represents the future.

Lay out the ten cards from the pile of the Past from left to right. Repeat with the Present and Future piles. Begin your interpretation with the Past cards, then the Present, then the Future, and look at the two Surprise cards last.

EXAMPLE

Pile 1: the past

Pile 2: the present

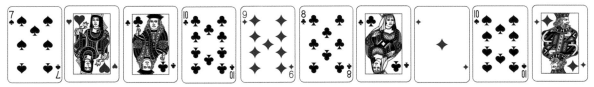

Pile 3: the future

*Reversed

See which suit is dominant. Hearts and Clubs are the most positive, while Diamonds and Spades are less so; Spades are generally associated with loss and great opposition, so at first glance, you get to see if a row of cards is generally positive or negative.

1 Look for patterns. Three Eights mean new family ties, while two Kings denote trustworthy partnerships. Note that we only look for duplicates within a row, not across all three rows.

2 Read the individual card meanings and put them together with what you already know. See if any cards are reversed, as these usually have a more negative meaning than upright cards.

3 Interpret the two Surprise cards.

If we were to interpret the row from pile 3, the future, we see that:

There are two Diamonds, four Spades, three Hearts, and one Club. As there are four Spades, the suit of misfortune, along with a mix of Diamonds and Hearts, the balance of cards revealing future influences are mixed; there are some positives and some challenges to overcome.

There are two Aces and two Eights. The two Aces represent a turbulent partnership, while the two Eights show flirtation and infatuation—so the questioner may begin a liaison with an unsuitable man or woman. The King and Queen of Spades may represent a married couple, so the flirtation or affair could be with the man or woman of this pair, explaining why it is unadvisable.

As there are no reversed cards in this row, the upright card meanings do not become intensified or negative, so are read individually. The Seven of Diamonds shows a social situation that should be taken lightly, and in combination with the Eight of Diamonds, means gossip and discovering its source. The Nine of Spades indicates stress. The Jack of Hearts suggests good company and romance. The last card, the Ten of Hearts, signifies eventual happiness after suffering. Putting this all together, the future cards suggest meeting a charismatic person socially, but it would be inadvisable to take this further given he or she may be married or otherwise committed. Otherwise, the liaison brings stress and gossip—but regardless of what the questioner chooses to do, he or she will make a better choice of partner eventually, signified by the delayed happiness of the Ten of Hearts.

The Surprise cards are the Jack of Spades reversed and the nine of Hearts. These cards may seem at odds with one another, but they tell a story and offer additional insight into the questioner's situation. The Jack of Spades shows a charming but deceitful character, while the Hearts card reveals a wish come true. This can be interpreted as reassurance that the questioner can have the relationship he or she desires and does not have to tolerate second best.

(For all the card meanings, see page 136.)

Insights and Answers: Thirteen Cards

This layout uses thirteen cards, arranged in five piles, each of which relates to a life area. You interpret the cards in each pile to pinpoint your situation, relationships, expectations, potential outcomes, and surprises in store so it's a great spread when you want to dig a little deeper or if you have further questions after a three-card reading.

Shuffle the deck, asking, "What do I need to know now?" and cut it once, making two piles of cards and placing the bottom pile on top. Next, lay all the cards out in a fan shape, facedown. Choose thirteen cards with your left hand and put the remainder of the deck to one side as you won't be needing it. Shuffle your chosen thirteen cards, cut them as you did before, then deal from the top of the pile. Lay them from right to left and then continue, so you have five piles of cards, as shown below.

So, you'll have two cards in piles 4 and 5 and three cards in piles 1, 2, and 3.

Life Area

Pile 5: Your situation.

Pile 4: Domestic life: love, relationships, friendships.

Pile 3: What you expect or hope for.

Pile 2: The surprise pile: unknown factors or influences.

Pile 1: The outcome.

Begin by interpreting pile 5, then pile 4, and so on, to finish with pile 1, the outcome. Look up the meanings of the two or three cards in each pile in turn and intuit how their meanings work together to offer a meaning (see page 136).

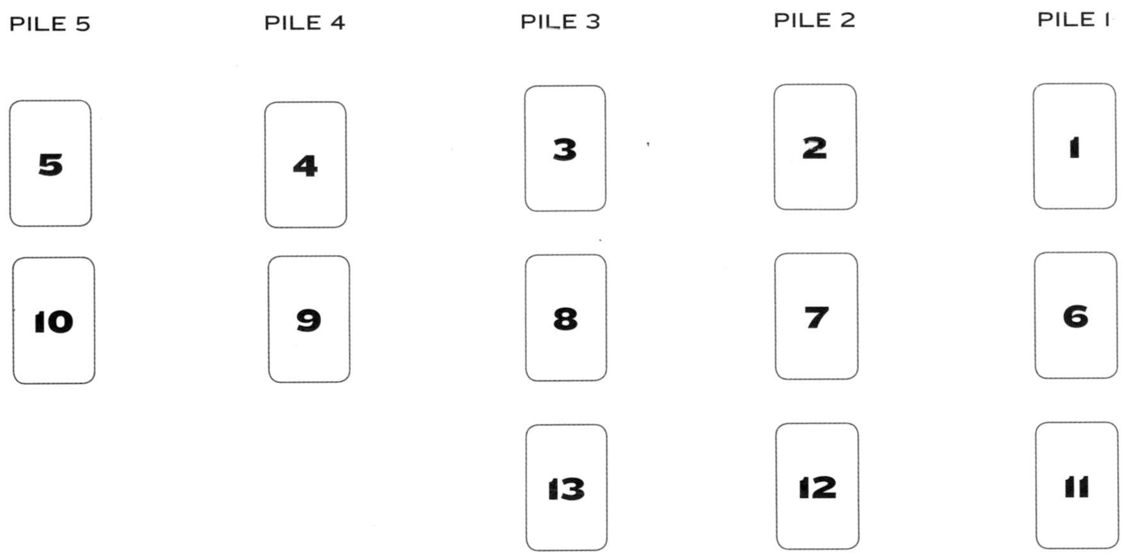

PILE 5	PILE 4	PILE 3	PILE 2	PILE I
5	4	3	2	1
10	9	8	7	6
		13	12	11

The Master Method

The Master Method, also known as the Square of Thirty-Six, uses thirty-six cards in a six-by-six grid, so you will need a large surface on which to lay out the cards. Each card position has an individual meaning, representing different life aspects, from relationships to health, prospects to worries, so it's a great method to use when you're ready to really examine current influences in detail. However, you will need a fair amount of time and a notebook to keep track of the card meanings.

If you prefer, you can adapt this method to focus on fewer cards. For example, if your question is about relationships, happiness, and security, you can just interpret the third row of cards numbered 13 through 18. Or choose a column: For example, column three focuses on work-related issues: success, business/work relationships, financial security, opposition, change, and neglect (the neglect card reveals what or who gets neglected). This card column helps you discern your success potential and if you've got your work-life balance right.

First, reduce the deck to thirty-six cards. To do this, take out all the Twos, Threes, Fours, and Fives, so you're left with all the Aces, Sixes, Sevens, Eights, Nines, Tens, Jacks, Queens, and Kings of each suit.

Shuffle and cut the deck and then lay them faceup, following the grid pattern shown to the right.

Look up the card meanings here and take a note of each one as you go to help you recall all their interpretations.

INTERPRETING THE CARDS THE EASY WAY

You will notice that the four suits as interpreted in this method tend to apply the same meaning to each card position, which you can use as a shortcut. These meanings apply just to this Master Method reading.

Hearts: Fulfillment and success.

Clubs: Supportive friends.

Diamonds: Blocks and jealousy.

Spades: Mistrust, loss, and deceit.

At first glance, note the cards' hierarchy: The King, Queen, Jack, Ten, and Ace (Ace is high) are believed to have more impact on your life than the Sixes, Sevens, Eights, or Nines of each suit.

Your plans 1	Potential achievement 2	Success 3	Expectations 4	Luck and risks 5	Hopes and wishes 6
Injustice 7	Others' ingratitude 8	Work/ business relationships 9	Setbacks 10	Trouble 11	Possessions and circumstances 12
Happiness 13	Love 14	Financial security 15	Committed relationships 16	Underlying worries 17	Harmony 18
Windfalls 19	Others' dishonesty 20	Opposition 21	Gifts 22	Friendships 23	Progress 24
Cooperation and kindness 25	Long-term projects 26	Change 27	Sorrow and bereavement 28	Appreciation 29	Scandal 30
Future opportunities 31	Money and prospects 32	Neglect 33	Support 34	Ambition 35	Health 36

1. YOUR PLANS

The card in this position reveals what is at the forefront of your mind. This may be a specific project or a direction you wish to take; it's often the reason for doing a reading.

Hearts: Your project is well starred and is highly likely to succeed.

Clubs: A Clubs card in this position shows you have support from friends to help you move a project or situation forward.

Diamonds: You may encounter delays and blocks that may also be financial.

Spades: You may be undermined, so be careful whom you confide in.

2. POTENTIAL ACHIEVEMENT

This card position reveals the outcome of your work and the potential benefits or challenges to success.

Hearts: Your hopes for success are well founded; your goals can be achieved.

Clubs: Friends care for you and support you in your goals.

Diamonds: Jealousy may disrupt your plans and progress, but you will succeed.

Spades: Deceit and underhandedness; beware of sly tactics.

3. SUCCESS

The Success position reveals recognition for your achievements and how you might fare.

Hearts: Great success and recognition for your efforts.

Clubs: Achievement through support from others, or success that is shared.

Diamonds: Minor or partial success; you will gain due recognition later.

Spades: Others' envy threatens your progress; they may resort to deviousness.

4. EXPECTATIONS

The Expectations position reveals what you currently expect to happen and how realistic your expectations are.

Hearts: Your expectations are well founded and will be met.

Clubs: Friends help you realize your goals; a Clubs card in this position also shows you have the determination to succeed.

Diamonds: You can expect more of yourself; you can achieve greater goals.

Spades: Your expectations may be too ambitious and even fantastical; set yourself a more realistic goal.

5. LUCK AND RISKS

This card position reveals your luck in general, along with financial investments and business risks; it also shows likely outcomes if you place a bet or chase up a debt.

Hearts: Luck is on your side; this is a good time to take a chance.

Clubs: Information from a reliable person leads to a win.

Diamonds: You lose and win; as your fortunes could go either way, recover any money owed to you now.

Spades: Dishonesty abounds, so do not take financial risks at present.

6. HOPES AND WISHES

The Hopes and Wishes position reveals what you truly desire, such as money or love, rather than what you expect to happen (as in position 4).

Hearts: Your desires will be almost immediately fulfilled.

Clubs: Influential people help you achieve some part of your wish, and you may need to accept that this is enough for now.

Diamonds: You will need to work hard for what you want; even with help from friends, it's unlikely you will be entirely satisfied with what you get.

Spades: You're unable to have your wishes granted at present.

7. INJUSTICE

The Injustice position reveals unfair treatment; it shows if it is worth seeking justice or if it is better to walk away.

Hearts: You receive an admission or an apology, and any accusation against you will be withdrawn; you may turn this situation to your advantage.

Clubs: It may take time to recover, but you will move on; friends will stand up for you and help put the situation right.

Diamonds: If you can forgive those who have wronged you, they will try to make amends.

Spades: Taking a perpetrator to task will make the situation worse; let it go.

8. OTHERS' INGRATITUDE

This card position highlights giving and envy and helps explain why your generosity is not acknowledged.

Hearts: You will receive thanks or respect from the people who matter to you; those who seem ungrateful are threatened by your achievements.

Clubs: Let go of your expectations; your acknowledgment will come at a later date.

Diamonds: You may need to investigate this situation further, as some people may have hidden agendas.

Spades: Those whom you have helped do not deserve it; save your generosity for the right people.

9. WORK/BUSINESS RELATIONSHIPS

This card position includes colleagues, clients, and other contacts involved in your day-to-day working life.

Hearts: Great working relationships bring financial profit and friendship.

Clubs: Work on clear communication to avoid misunderstandings.

Diamonds: Aim for good relationships with everyone rather than favor just a few.

Spades: A toxic environment or network means you cannot trust those you work with.

10. SETBACKS

Setbacks refers to potential losses in friendships, finances, and status.

Hearts: A close and supportive friend leaves your circle.

Clubs: A friend's absence leaves a gap in your life.

Diamonds: The loss of money or material goods; take extra care of your finances and possessions.

Spades: Be very careful whom you trust, as Spades in this position can indicate a threat to your position; you may have to change direction.

11. TROUBLE

Trouble includes personal problems and issues that may affect your work, but the focus is mainly on love, friends, and family.

Hearts: A dispute between close relatives needs immediate attention.

Clubs: Quarrels between friends may fracture a group.

Diamonds: Arguments about money and/or responsibilities.

Spades: Disagreements arise from envy.

12. POSSESSIONS AND CIRCUMSTANCES

The card in the Possessions position reveals your material wealth and security, from your home to money saved or invested.

Hearts: A gradual, steady improvement in your lifestyle.

Clubs: Slow progress; hard work and friends ensure you're moving in the right direction.

Diamonds: You need to deal with blocks and opposition now rather than wait; a Diamond in this position can also show problems with property.

Spades: Your circumstances may be getting worse rather than better; change your goal to find a more productive way ahead.

13. HAPPINESS

The card in the Happiness position reveals what brings you joy.

Hearts: Ideas and feeling inspired uplifts you; good living also brings you pleasure.

Clubs: Financial security brings you joy and comfort.

Diamonds: Hard-won success is your happiness key; winning against the odds brings you great satisfaction.

Spades: Happiness comes from helping others, which may also bring you acknowledgment and rewards.

14. LOVE

This is a significant card in the layout, as the nature of the romance you have now or will have in the future can affect your outlook on life in general.

Hearts: You are, or will be, blessed with love.

Clubs: Loyalty and trust make your relationship solid and loving; you can rely on your partner completely.

Diamonds: The relationship may be undermined by jealousy; also, your lifestyles may be very different; this love will take work.

Spades: In an existing relationship, there is irritation and doubt; a new potential partner may offer you more.

15. FINANCIAL SECURITY

The card in this position shows your financial trend—whether you are likely to prosper or struggle.

Hearts: Well-deserved prosperity; Hearts also say you benefit from luck.

Clubs: You may feel worn down, but you can succeed; friends can help you.

Diamonds: Jealousy gets in the way of your progress; do not let others' envy disrupt your goals or upset you.

Spades: Envious people may campaign against you; confront this now.

16. COMMITTED RELATIONSHIPS

This card position is traditionally named marriage, but here it has been adapted to include all committed partnerships.

Hearts: A happy relationship based on empathy and mutual interests; if the Ace of Hearts lands here, a happy future is forecast.

Clubs: Friendship turns to love; there will also be a strong practical or financial aspect to the relationship.

Diamonds: One or both partners feel insecure and/or jealous.

Spades: Deceit, infidelity, and suspicion; traditionally, if the Seven, Eight, or Nine of Spades appears in this position, separation may be a possibility.

17. UNDERLYING WORRIES

The card in this position represents anxieties and worries we may keep hidden from others, but that can at times dominate our thoughts.

Hearts: Relationship problems are soon overcome.

Clubs: An argument with a close friend or within a group is distressing, but you can forgive and forget.

Diamonds: Jealousy causes unhappiness; also, there may be a simple misunderstanding; be calm.

Spades: If you are feeling attacked, criticized, or betrayed, do not be drawn into a confrontation; step away.

18. HARMONY

The interpretations here focus on cultivating harmony through good relationships with those around you.

Hearts: Stay true to your friends when a new romance distracts you.

Clubs: Value the people who have helped you over the years; they are your true friends.

Diamonds: Loyalty is important now as friends may need your unwavering support.

Spades: If friends demand much more than they give, it is time to seek new ones.

19. WINDFALLS

Windfalls include sudden winnings, bonuses, and inheritance—any income that is unearned or unexpected.

Hearts: You come into a large sum of money or a great opportunity comes your way.

Clubs: Money coming from a friend or a group, such as a charity.

Diamonds: Disputes over inheritance or other unexpected income; you may need to compromise on your share.

Spades: Missing out on deserved money due to fraud or unfair challenges to your position.

20. OTHERS' DISHONESTY

The card in the Others' Dishonesty position covers fraud and, in general, people who cannot be trusted who have not yet been exposed.

Hearts: A deceitful person is caught out; let them take responsibility for their dishonesty.

Clubs: Friends alert you to possible deception and help protect you; you may also seek professional advice.

Diamonds: You may have to suffer someone's attempt at wrongdoing, but they will not get far; sit tight.

Spades: The impact of deception is unfortunately unavoidable.

21. OPPOSITION

Opposition in this card position means obvious and external conflict, particularly rivals in love, business, or other situations involving competition.

Hearts: Your opponents will not win, and you will succeed.

Clubs: You have the support of friends around you, and you are protected.

Diamonds: A rival will try hard to get their own way but will only partially succeed.

Spades: Your antagonist has the upper hand; it is better to accept defeat rather than fight on.

22. GIFTS

Gifts include any present you receive, from small tokens of affection to grander displays of thanks.

Hearts: You receive a wonderful gift that expresses deep gratitude or love.

Clubs: Useful gifts from friends or relatives.

Diamonds: Gifts that put you under an obligation or are unwanted.

Spades: A present or favor designed to buy or bribe you.

23. FRIENDSHIPS

The card in the Friendships position reveals how much you can rely upon others.

Hearts: Faithful friends have great affection for you.

Clubs: Friends may not be perfect, but they are loyal and have your best interests at heart.

Diamonds: A high-maintenance group of friends; keeping them happy takes effort.

Spades: Needy and unreliable friends who are hard to trust.

24. PROGRESS

This card position reveals how you might increase your status and improve your standard of living.

Hearts: A sudden step up, promotion, or other great improvement to your position.

Clubs: Hard work brings rewards; others are impressed by your abilities.

Diamonds: You may struggle with criticism, but with resilience you can succeed.

Spades: With determination, you can overcome obstacles and rivalry, but the journey will be hard.

25. COOPERATION AND KINDNESS

This card position shows the possibility of being treated kindly by people around you and how much to reach out to others.

Hearts: Great support and advice arrives just when you need it.

Clubs: Ask for help and you will receive it; whatever support you need is there, but you do need to ask rather than assume it will come.

Diamonds: You receive some support, but this may not be consistent; accept what is available.

Spades: You will need to help yourself; others may not be able to assist you now, even if their intentions are good.

26. LONG-TERM PROJECTS

This card position covers long-term projects and goals at work and home, and it shows how you might succeed.

Hearts: Ultimate success; you may decide to extend your goal and aim for even greater achievement.

Clubs: Friends support you, but you need to be diligent and self-directed, too.

Diamonds: Others use the project to further their own reputation.

Spades: You may need to wait rather than forge ahead; there are many obstacles in your way just now.

27. CHANGE

This card position refers to major changes you want to make or how to deal with a change that is offered to you, such as relocation or a new role at work.

Hearts: You can choose not to make a change if you are happy with your situation now; if not, an opportunity is coming soon.

Clubs: Carefully investigate all the options and seek advice before you make your decision.

Diamonds: Avoid making a major change just now, as it could lead to disagreements and frustration.

Spades: The change offered to you will not lead to fulfillment; hold your ground.

28. SORROW AND BEREAVEMENT

This card position includes bereavement and other losses, such as a close friend or relative moving away.

Hearts: The loss or bereavement brings a deep lesson, and you may receive something that is of sentimental or material value.

Clubs: The loss or death of a friend.

Diamonds: A shock departure or loss of a friend or relative.

Spades: An unexpected loss or bereavement makes a situation clear and may actually resolve a situation or problem.

29. APPRECIATION

The card in this position shows rewards and appreciation for long-term work and effort.

Hearts: A great reward, far beyond your expectations.

Clubs: You are appreciated and rewarded for hard work; you are well regarded by friends and colleagues.

Diamonds: You receive acknowledgment for your efforts, but this triggers envy in the less successful people around you.

Spades: Dishonest people claim credit for some of the work you have done, so you are underappreciated.

30. SCANDAL

This card position refers to misfortune, gossip, and any potential damage to your reputation.

Hearts: A problem will be short-lived; you will not be affected or hurt by rumors.

Clubs: The Six, Seven, Eight, or Nine of Clubs means a personal secret is exposed; the Ace, King, Queen, or Jack shows the scandal concerns a friend but affects you, too.

Diamonds: Jealousy drives an attack on your reputation; step back and allow this envy to burn out rather than get involved.

Spades: A difficult time, even when dealing with false accusations.

31. FUTURE OPPORTUNITIES

The card in this position reveals potential future influences.

Hearts: Wonderful good luck that brings long-lasting contentment and success.

Clubs: A great opportunity comes through friends and contacts; someone may put your name forward.

Diamonds: Challenges and jealous opposition make no difference to your good prospects and may even make you stronger.

Spades: Great difficulties cause stress, but you do have support, and you will endure and thrive.

32. MONEY AND PROSPECTS

The card in this position offers predictions, along with advice on managing and keeping money when you have it.

Hearts: You have the potential to be wealthy through luck, inheritance, a windfall, or work.

Clubs: Nurture your network of friends and colleagues, work hard, and money will come.

Diamonds: Invest your money wisely and do not lend too much to friends; you may not get it back.

Spades: Effort does not lead to the money you deserve; it will come but will take its time. Also, be alert to dishonest practices and people.

33. NEGLECT

The card in this position refers to things in life that are being neglected and need attention.

Hearts: Insensitivity or indifference to others' feelings while you climb the ladder of ambition.

Clubs: Neglecting friends; get in touch before they drift away from you.

Diamonds: Look after your possessions and your own interests; otherwise, you may be taken advantage of.

Spades: You may already have suffered due to a lack of care or interest in your possessions and emotional well-being; take action to prevent further loss.

34. SUPPORT

The card in this position reveals the likelihood of getting help, favors, and other support.

Hearts: Wealthy people favor you and promote your interests.

Clubs: A wide network of friends supports and helps you.

Diamonds: You may need to compete for attention and support, so be wary of people who want to take from you rather than give.

Spades: Try not to expect favors or support, as this is unlikely to materialize at present.

35. AMBITION

The Ambition position advises how best to work toward your goals.

Hearts: Keep pursuing your ambition; you will soon achieve a great goal.

Clubs: You succeed through leading a group; you have their respect.

Diamonds: You may need to keep an ambition secret to avoid attracting jealousy.

Spades: Rethink your direction, as your current track may not be right for you; see this as an opportunity to let go of an unrealistic goal.

36. HEALTH

Health encompasses potential ailments and illnesses. Please note that these traditional interpretations dealt with health conditions in a way we may consider inappropriate today. You may prefer to interpret these cards as how we respond to stress and pressure, rather than as health warnings.

Hearts: A brief ailment or illness from which you quickly recover.

Clubs: A possible illness.

Diamonds: A minor condition, most likely a recurring ailment.

Spades: A longer-term condition or illness that takes time to heal.

PLAYING-CARD **MEANINGS**

The card meanings that follow reflect universal concerns. However, you will see that there is emphasis on some negative issues, such as gossip and jealousy or portents of illness. And of course, there's the gender divide: Groups of Kings in a reading denote business and success, whereas groups of Queens signify socializing and gossip. However, on a positive note, these card meanings are free from the psychological interpretations and say exactly what they mean—perfect when you need a direct answer to a question. Also, as you progress from the simpler layouts to using more cards, many more interpretative possibilities arise. By looking at a greater number of possibilities, you'll find you naturally intuit new card connections and meanings that are unique to you.

The Suit of Hearts

The suit of Hearts focuses on emotions and love, romance and relationships, friendships, home life, socializing, and gaining your heart's desire in other aspects of your life.

ACE OF HEARTS

This Ace signifies a new beginning and good news, particularly in love, often after a broken relationship or a period of stress or disinterest. Falling in love with a new partner, finding a new friend or home, or finding a creative outlet that you wholeheartedly pursue.

Reversed meaning: Loss or disappointment.

KING OF HEARTS

A sociable, mature man with high emotional intelligence, this King makes an excellent friend and adviser; he listens carefully rather than making judgments and assumptions.
Appreciating the best things in life, he is a bon vivant known for his generosity.

Reversed meaning: A pushy and mean-spirited individual.

With the Nine of Hearts: A love wish comes true.

QUEEN OF HEARTS

A mature, honest, and loving woman who gives more than she takes, this Queen is usually married or in a committed relationship. In a man's reading, the card represents his existing partner or the qualities he desires in an ideal future partner.

Reversed meaning: Relationship blocks.

JACK OF HEARTS

This Jack is a youthful or young-at-heart individual who is good company. An additional meaning is a friendship that evolves into a light-hearted romance. This person makes you feel younger than your years.

Reversed meaning: A relationship rift that needs healing, past or present.

TEN OF HEARTS

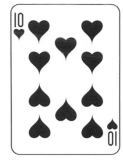

Everything gets better with this Ten; old issues and burdens disappear, and you feel happy and fulfilled. Additional meanings include children or taking a trip with a great companion, whether lover or friend.

Reversed meaning: Great happiness, temporarily delayed; overall, the upright meaning stands.

With the Ace of Diamonds: Marriage, celebrations, blessings, happiness.

With the Ten of Spades: A gradual improvement; there may be some issues to resolve along the way.

NINE OF HEARTS

The wish-come-true card: A dearly held wish will be granted. It is also the card of manifesting and says that whatever you set your heart on now can come to you. The card also brings wealth, celebrations, and happy surprises.

Reversed meaning: The happiness of the upright card will come, but after a short interval of stress or sadness.

With the King of Hearts: A love wish comes true.

With the Nine of Clubs: An inheritance.

With the Ten of Spades: Delay or temporary blocks to progress.

EIGHT OF HEARTS

The Eight brings balance and order; there are no major highs or lows, and everything flows naturally. Relationships are stable and content, and you may be considering making a love commitment.

Reversed meaning: Inability to get a relationship on an even keel; alternatively, unrequited love or a lack of affection from an existing partner.

With the Eight of Diamonds: A journey and a celebration.

SEVEN OF HEARTS

The card is traditionally associated with marriage, true love, and happiness; additional meanings include choices, so your decision is likely to concern love and relationships. In creative projects, this Seven brings lots of possible ways to express ideas.

Reversed meaning: Boredom or creative blocks; jealousy in relationships; affairs.

The Suit of Clubs

The suit of Clubs focuses on communication, personal growth, health, travel, and worldly desires, such as business or creative success.

ACE OF CLUBS

This Ace brings success, money, well-being, and new opportunities. You are energized and poised to drive forward a new project, enterprise, or creative idea. New partnerships and love relationships are also favored now.

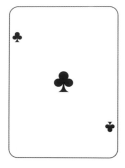

Reversed meaning: Love does not suffer when this Ace reverses, but communication problems mean some projects go on hold.

With the Seven of Diamonds and Seven of Clubs: Great prosperity.

KING OF CLUBS

A friendly, loyal, and straightforward man, this King has a direct manner; what you see is what you get. He is usually well connected and moves in influential circles. He makes a good friend and will protect your interests.

Reversed meaning: An individual whose self-doubt sabotages his goals.

QUEEN OF CLUBS

A mature, confident, and passionate woman, this Queen thrives on new opportunities; she has great energy and makes an inspiring leader and manager. She needs to express herself and communicates well with others.

Reversed meaning: An unreliable and selfish individual.

JACK OF CLUBS

A young person, or a person young at heart, this high-energy Jack loves the excitement of the new. As a friend or lover, he or she is loyal and trustworthy. This Jack could have a special talent or skill and may excel at sport.

Reversed meaning: An insincere, and potentially dangerous, individual.

TEN OF CLUBS

This Ten brings money, luck, and travel, so you may enjoy a well-deserved holiday or time out from work and usual responsibilities to enjoy material wealth. Business dealings and projects receive an unexpected boost.

Reversed meaning: An immediate need to escape from trouble or pressure; an additional meaning is legal issues and problems with authority.

With the Ace of Clubs, Diamonds, or Hearts: A windfall.

With the Nine of Diamonds: Delays to plans; a period of waiting.

With the Nine of Spades: The good fortune of the Ten is canceled by this negative card.

NINE OF CLUBS

This happy Nine brings gifts, such as unexpected money. In love, there will be a great opportunity for a new relationship in the future. Existing relationships are close and fulfilling.

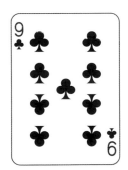

Reversed meaning: Gifts and love will come but will take a little more time to manifest.

With the Nine of Hearts: An inheritance.

EIGHT OF CLUBS

This Eight can show a need for money, as more cash flows in than out. However, this is traditionally a good card for relationships; at present, you just can't have a great love life and complete financial security at the same time.

Reversed meaning: You may invest too much too soon in a relationship or financial venture.

With the Eight of Diamonds: Love that lasts.

With the Ten of Diamonds: A journey motivated by love.

SEVEN OF CLUBS

This Seven shows financial success. You may also recover money, as a debt is repaid; you will learn from this experience. An additional meaning of the card is children and youthfulness.

Reversed meaning: Irritations and money worries.

With the Ace of Clubs and Seven of Diamonds: Great prosperity.

The Suit of Diamonds

The suit of Diamonds focuses on the physical world—home and property, finances, and practical needs.

ACE OF DIAMONDS

An important document, email, or letter is coming to you. This Ace can also represent an award or gift that will bring you great happiness. A traditional meaning of the card also includes a ring or marriage proposal.

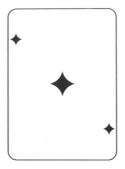

Reversed meaning: Unwelcome news regarding finances and business; debt.

With the Nine of Diamonds and Ten of Diamonds: Important news; if followed by a Court card, a necessary journey.

With the Seven of Diamonds: Good news you can rely upon.

With the Ten of Hearts: Marriage, celebrations, blessings, happiness.

KING OF DIAMONDS

This wise King provides a stable home and income and is very protective of those he loves. Happier being physically active, he may not be a great communicator, but his intentions are honorable. It is important to him to be of service, and his career choice may reflect this.

Reversed meaning: A moody, scheming individual.

QUEEN OF DIAMONDS

A mature woman, usually married or in a long-term relationship, this Queen offers solid support and advice. She may be rather literal in her outlook, but she is an expert problem-solver who gets things done.

Reversed meaning: A jealous and untrustworthy individual.

With the Seven of Diamonds: Important decisions; focused effort.

JACK OF DIAMONDS

This Jack usually represents a person acting in an official capacity. He or she may be a messenger, offering advice, or you may help him in some way. However you connect, the interaction is positive.

Reversed meaning: An arrogant, deceitful individual.

TEN OF DIAMONDS

This Ten brings happiness in love, and marriage is one of the card's traditional meanings. Money and financial security beckon, too, and possibly a new home in a new location.

Reversed meaning:

Misfortune; decisions that lead to unhappiness or stress.

With the Nine and Ace of Diamonds: Important news; if followed by a Court card, a necessary journey.

With the Eight of Clubs: A journey motivated by love.

With the Seven of Spades: Delay and irritation.

NINE OF DIAMONDS

This Nine shows blocks to your plans, causing disappointment and even anxiety. However, the delay is often for good reason, as some truths come to light, so you may decide to make better alternative arrangements. Another traditional meaning of the card is news.

Reversed meaning: Quarrels in relationships; money stress.

With the Ace and Ten of Diamonds: Important news; if followed by a Court card, a journey will be necessary.

EIGHT OF DIAMONDS

Love and affection are expressed, face to face or through emails, texts, and messages. Other traditional meanings of the card include short trips away and a young, professional person.

Reversed meaning: Disappointment in love; rejection of affection.

With the Eight of Hearts: A journey and a celebration.

With the Eight of Clubs: Love that lasts.

With the Seven of Diamonds: Gossip; you discover the culprit.

SEVEN OF DIAMONDS

The Seven brings light-hearted conversation with no serious or meaningful intentions. There may be gossip or casual criticism. Another traditional meaning is a child.

Reversed meaning:

Scandal or heavy, unfair criticism; possible issues with children.

With the Ace of Diamonds: Good news you can rely upon.

With the Queen of Diamonds: Important decisions; focused effort.

With the Eight of Diamonds: Discovering the source of gossip.

With the Ace of Clubs and Seven of Clubs: Great prosperity.

The Suit of Spades

The suit of Spades focuses on life's challenges—loss, fear, and disappointment.

ACE OF SPADES

This Ace signifies loss and sorrow. There may be unwanted news, such as a legal challenge or ruling against you or an organization; additional traditional meanings include deception and betrayal.

Reversed meaning: The upright meaning, as above, along with errors of judgment.

KING OF SPADES

A difficult, overbearing man, this King is often critical and overly opinionated. In love relationships, however, he can be attentive and reliable. Another traditional meaning of the card is a professional man

with social standing, such as a lawyer, business owner, or doctor.

Reversed meaning: A dangerous adversary; the negative character traits of the upright card are intensified.

QUEEN OF SPADES

This Queen is a bitter or deeply resentful woman who may try to be a friend but does not have the capacity to be genuine: the ultimate frenemy.

Reversed meaning: An individual who thrives on drama; spiteful behavior.

JACK OF SPADES

This Jack is a tactless younger person who often prefers to provoke other people rather than genuinely engage with them. He is capable of decent behavior and can be entertaining, but it may be tough to ignore his lack of sensitivity.

Reversed meaning: A flatterer who is out to deceive.

TEN OF SPADES

Unfortunately, this Ten is regarded as the most difficult in the deck, as it signifies grief, stress, and one challenge after another, leaving you feeling bewildered and constantly beset by troubles. Another traditional meaning is taking a long trip away.

Reversed meaning: Given the upright meaning, there is no reversed meaning for this card.

With the Nine or Ten of Hearts: Some of your problems will be lessened or resolved.

NINE OF SPADES

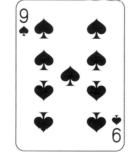

This Nine traditionally heralds bad news concerning finances, relationships, well-being, or business affairs.

Reversed meaning: The reversed meaning of the Nine is even more severe than the upright meaning. Look for the Ten of Hearts in your reading, as this signifies freedom from troubles.

EIGHT OF SPADES

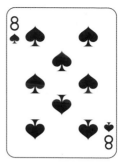

Pay attention to your health and well-being. Another traditional meaning is unwelcome news.

Reversed meaning: A broken relationship.

With the Seven of Diamonds: A deeper emphasis on avoiding potential health issues.

SEVEN OF SPADES

This Seven signifies anxiety and negative thinking patterns that may be habitual rather than appropriate.

Reversed meaning: Ideas that could lead to impulsive, ill-advised actions.

With the Ten of Diamonds: Better times are ahead, but there may be a frustrating wait.

With a Court card: A false friend.

Card Combinations

FOUR ACES

Four Aces bring a clash of power in the form of financial setbacks, relationship quarrels, and dangerous tension. If some of the Aces are reversed, the impact is less disruptive. An extended meaning of the power clash of the Aces is a significant change or new surroundings.

THREE ACES

Three upright Aces signify troubles and challenges, but they are short-lived; positive news is on the way. An alternative reading of this triplet is infidelity. If the Aces are reversed, be sure that your behavior is not insensitive, unreasonable, or otherwise excessive.

TWO ACES

Two Aces reveal togetherness. The Ace of Hearts with the Ace of Clubs foretells happiness and good fortune. If Diamonds and Spades come together, the relationship could be fraught with drama. If one or both Aces are reversed, the partnership will struggle to thrive.

FOUR KINGS

The combination of four Kings is positive; this quartet brings success and business progress, along with acknowledgment of your work, which may come as a reward or award. If all the Kings are reversed, the honors come more quickly, but they will be less significant.

THREE KINGS

Three Kings bring reassurance that an urgent or stressful situation will be addressed. If any appears reversed, the situation is more complicated than you had assumed and will take more time to unravel and resolve. If all three Kings are reversed, there are too many challenges; reconsider your goal.

TWO KINGS

Two Kings signify a productive and honest business or creative partnership. If one of the Kings is reversed, there will be one obstacle, but you will be motivated to resolve it. If both Kings are reversed, two obstacles can be overcome.

FOUR QUEENS

Four Queens represent a social gathering. If any of the Queens is reversed, a social gathering is spoiled.

THREE QUEENS

Three Queens denote friendly visitors who bring good news. If all three Queens are reversed, there's a dangerous edge to gossip and the possibility of scandal.

TWO QUEENS

Two Queens see two friends getting together. Secrets are told, and if either Queen is reversed, a confidence will be betrayed. One Queen reversed means rivalry between them. If both Queens are reversed, the questioner suffers due to his own actions.

FOUR JACKS

Four Jacks bring a sociable gathering, but youthful high spirits may escalate into competitiveness and pointless argument. If one or more Jacks are reversed, the situation is less likely to escalate. An alternative meaning is tradespeople or agents coming to the house.

THREE JACKS

Three Jacks signify grievances with friends and at worst, deceit. If one or more Jacks are reversed, the situation is not serious; only brief irritation is foretold.

TWO JACKS

If the Jack of Hearts and Jack of Clubs appear in a reading, there could be a personality clash and trouble as a result. Any other pairing of Jacks is considered problematic, too, bringing underhand schemes and loss. If both Jacks are reversed, this situation may be upon the questioner now; one Jack reversed slows down the time frame.

FOUR TENS

Four tens bring good fortune, prosperity, and success in whatever you do. One reversed Ten signifies one obstacle to success; two reversed cards denote two obstacles, and so on. Pinpoint these blocks, and you may be able to see solutions to each one.

THREE TENS

Traditionally, three Tens show a legal action against you, but you can interpret this more generally as strong opposition in any life area. Reversals bring help, so the more reversed Tens you have, the stronger your position.

TWO TENS

Two Tens are a sign of luck, which may be linked with your work or creative projects; you may find a new career direction. One reversed card says this change will come soon, maybe within a few weeks; if both are reversed, this change is much further in the future. A further interpretation is that the red Tens together—the Ten of Hearts with the Ten of Diamonds—foretell a wedding.

FOUR NINES

Four Nines together show a welcome surprise. The more Nines that are reversed, the longer the surprise takes to manifest.

THREE NINES

Three Nines reveal happiness, prosperity, and well-being. If all the Nines that are reversed, some financial glitches get in the way; after these are resolved, good fortune comes.

TWO NINES

Two Nines denote happiness in relationships and success in a business or creative enterprise. An additional meaning is moving home. The Nine of Clubs with the Nine of Hearts signifies an inheritance. If one or both Nines are reversed, there may be minor problems or worries, but these do not detract from the overall success foretold by the card.

FOUR EIGHTS

Four Eights signify some successes and some failures, particularly in relation to travel and new jobs. If all the Eights are reversed, calmness and stability prevail.

THREE EIGHTS

Three Eights denote new family ties. This may be due to a wedding, other love commitment, or the birth of a baby. If all the Eights are reversed, this suggests folly and self-indulgence.

TWO EIGHTS

Two Eights suggest infatuation, flirtation, and lightheartedness. The card also foretells a nice surprise or development. The Eight of Diamonds with the Eight of Hearts signifies a journey and a celebration; the Eight of Diamonds with the Eight of Clubs brings love that lasts. If both Eights are reversed, foolish actions may lead to unwelcome consequences.

FOUR SEVENS

Four Sevens show secret opposition; trouble comes from those who scheme against you. If all the Sevens are reversed, you may be unnerved by this discovery, but your opponents cannot do serious harm.

THREE SEVENS

Three Sevens signify loss of friends, along with regret and possible guilt. When reversed, the card's meaning is physical rather than emotional—you suffer minor ailments in reaction to something enjoyable, such as rich food or alcohol.

TWO SEVENS

Two Sevens bring a happy, unexpected event, and mutual love grows into a lasting relationship. If both Sevens are reversed, the card denotes infidelity, regret, and guilt.

A SEQUENCE OF COURT CARDS

Celebrations, friendship, and socializing.

A SEQUENCE OF SPADES

Money losses, discontentment, and jealousy.

A COURT CARD PLACED BETWEEN TWO CARDS OF THE SAME NUMBER

Restriction; the same-number cards oppose the Court card.

READING TAROT CARDS

Tarot is for insight, guidance, inspiration, self-understanding, healing, and prediction. Working with tarot is one of the greatest gifts you can give yourself because the cards, with their rich symbols, colors, and archetypal images, connect you with your inner guidance—and your own life story.

Painters were commissioned to create tarot cards in the courts of northern Italy as early as 1415. These gold-stamped, painted cards were royal family albums—one deck, painted for the Duke of Milan, commemorated the 1441 marriage of Bianca Maria Visconti to Francesco Sforza, whose likenesses were shown in The Lovers card. Divination came much later, with the occultist movement of the late eighteenth century. The early twentieth century saw the publication of the most influential deck of our times, the Rider Waite, from A. E. Waite, a member of the Hermetic Order of the Golden Dawn, a British occult society. Illustrated by Pamela Colman Smith, the deck is commonly referred to now as Rider Waite Smith.

There are now myriad decks available, and it's important to choose a deck that calls to you. This might be a witchy tarot, an angel tarot, a faerie tarot, a vampire deck, or a power-animal or cat tarot. You might find an artist online who paints limited editions of their own tarots, browse a catalog from one of the big card producers, or covet a friend's deck and buy your own. Finding the right deck for you sets you on your tarot path.

The tarot presented in these pages is the Universal Waite, which presents Colman Smith's drawings recolored by Mary Hanson-Roberts.

THE RIDER WAITE SMITH DECK

Many contemporary decks follow the imagery of the RWS, which includes full illustration for the minor arcana cards. The earlier tarots—such as the Visconti Sforzas and the Marseilles—have repeat patterns for the minors, like playing cards, whereas RWS-style cards include a full scene. These added details make interpretation easier, particularly for beginners.

The tarot deck comprises seventy-eight cards, divided into two groups, or arcana (arcana means "secret"). There are twenty-two major arcana cards, which can also be referred to as trumps or keys, and fifty-six minor arcana cards, arranged into four suits.

The twenty-two cards of the major arcana represent key turning points and decisions. If you're a beginner, it can help to interpret the major arcana cards in your spread first, then move to the minors, as you'll get the heart of the matter first. The majors are also a cycle, beginning with 0 The Fool, a beginning, and ending with XXI The World, or completion. The cards form a circle, known as the journey of The Fool, who travels through life physically and spiritually and is reborn with the World before he begins his journey again at zero. In this way, the numbers of the major arcana cards can show you where you are in any life phase. For example, if card XX Judgment comes up in a reading, you're coming to the end of that phase and looking back to the past before moving on. Cards with lower numbers, such as I or II, can give you the additional meaning of a new or young situation.

The fifty-six minor arcana cards are divided into four suits: Cups, Pentacles (or Coins), Wands (or Staves), and Swords. The suits may vary depending on your deck, but in most cases, each suit will relate to one of the four elements of Water, Earth, Fire, and Air.

- Cups cards take the element of Water. They represent emotions, love, relationships, imagination, and sensitivity.

- Pentacles cards take the element of Earth. They deal with physical reality—the material world and the body, home, money, security, and work.

- Wands take the element of Fire. They signify passion, communication, desire, creativity, and inspiration. Wands show there's lots of movement, activity, and talking.

- Swords take the element of Air. They reflect the mind—thought, analysis, and decisions. Swords can show there's opposition and ego around and sometimes, fear.

The Court cards are the Page, Knight, Queen, and King of each suit. They can be interpreted as people or as situations. For example, the Queen of Swords signifies independence and strength; you may have a manager or friend like this, or find that this is a message for you suggesting an approach you might take.

- Pages represent young people or young situations, such as an application for a new job or a budding new idea.

- Knights represent action. The Knights of Wands and Swords take fast action, as they're from the suits of Fire and Air, while the Knight of Cups is less forceful, as his suit is Water, for emotions and sensitivity. The Knight of Pentacles is slower and more considered in his approach, as his element is Earth.

- Queens and Kings represent achievement; a King and a Queen in the same spread can signify a couple, particularly if these cards fall close to each other.

HOW TO **BEGIN**

1 Find a quiet space with a clean, flat surface. Prepare a space for your readings where you will not be disturbed.

2 If you are working with a new deck, sort your cards into their arcanum and suits. If they come supplied in order, touch each card in turn as you look at each image. This creates a physical link with every card. Holding your cards, set an intention that you are energetically connected to them and that your readings are for the highest good. If you prefer, you can make a fan of the cards and hold it to your heart (with the card backs on the outside of the fan) and then set your intention.

3 Protect your cards when not in use by wrapping them in a reading cloth—a piece of fabric you lay the cards on when you read. Don't allow other people to handle them casually, as this confuses or dilutes their energy.

SHUFFLING **YOUR QUESTION INTO THE CARDS**

As you shuffle the deck, think of your question, imagining that your cards are absorbing the words. You can ask an open question such as, "What do I need to see/know today?" or make a request: "Tell me about *x* situation." Repeat your question out loud or in your mind as you shuffle; stop when you are ready.

If you're reading for someone else: Hand the deck to the person you are reading for—the questioner, or querent. Ask them to shuffle, thinking of their question or situation as they do so, and then return the deck to you.

READING THE NUMBERS

The numbers of the minors are a great key to interpretation. You can take the broad meaning of a card number and interpret it in terms of its suit. For example, a Six in any suit gives you the starting point of "harmony"; in the fiery suit of Wands, this indicates success, while in the quarrelsome suit of Swords, it sees you moving on from conflict.

- ▸ **Ace:** Beginnings
- ▸ **Two:** Partnerships, decisions
- ▸ **Three:** Acknowledgment, activity
- ▸ **Four:** Stability
- ▸ **Five:** Instability
- ▸ **Six:** Harmony, improvement
- ▸ **Seven:** Potential, ambition
- ▸ **Eight:** Gateways, change
- ▸ **Nine:** Intensity
- ▸ **Ten:** Completion

JUMPING CARDS

Jumping cards are those that appear to jump out of the deck during shuffling. Always look at a jumping card because it often reveals the theme of the reading. For example, the Ten of Wands would suggest feeling overwhelmed and lacking perspective. If you are reading for someone else, ask to see the jump card, make a mental note of it, and then ask the questioner to shuffle it back into the deck.

CHOOSING CARDS
FOR A SPREAD

There are three ways to do this:

1 Cutting the deck. Take the deck in your left hand and make three piles. Choose one pile, pick it up, and gather the remaining two piles under it, working from left to right. You're now ready to begin your tarot spread by dealing the cards from the top of the deck.

If you're reading for someone else: Ask them to make three piles with their left hand, choose a pile, and then gather the remaining two piles under it as before. Take back the deck and hold it facedown, ready to deal the cards from the top of the pile.

2 Fanning the cards. Spread all the cards facedown in a fan shape and choose, with your left hand, the number of cards you'll need for your spread.

If you're reading for someone else: Fan out the cards and ask them to choose the cards for the reading with their left hand and then pass each card to you in turn to lay out in your spread.

3 Any way you like. Choose your cards at random, plucking a card from any place in the deck.

READING THE CUT OF THE DECK

You can give a meaning to a chosen pile of cards before a reading begins. If your questioner chooses to put his left-hand pile of a cut deck on top, he is thinking of the past; if the center pile is chosen, he wants to know more about his present situation; and if he selects the right-hand pile, his focus is on future events.

REVERSED CARDS

Every card has an upright meaning and a reversed meaning; for most cards, the reversed meaning is a negative interpretation of the upright meaning.

Cards become reversed during shuffling; we can subconsciously do this during shuffling and cutting the deck. You can choose to read the reversed meanings of the cards, but many readers prefer to turn any reversed cards in a layout the right way up and read them all upright.

When you turn your cards faceup to begin a reading, turn them side to side, rather than flipping them upside down. Otherwise, your upright cards will appear reversed, and vice versa, which affects their meaning.

A FIRST READING:
ESSENTIAL TECHNIQUES

For this reading, we ask, "What do I need to see?" The cards will reveal the key influences around you now. Reading a small number of cards without laying them in a defined spread offers a way for you to interpret them freely. You'll get to see relationships between the majors and minors, and you'll notice patterns, such as cards with the same number or suit. These are the essential techniques of the professional reader. As you practice, you will find that your intuitive response to the cards steps in, and you do not need to consciously think about technique. These examples, therefore, are starting points, a way to activate your creativity and intuition in ways that will make your readings unique to you.

Choose four cards from the deck and shuffle them, making your request to see whatever is important now, and then choose your cards: Cut the deck, lay the cards out in a fan shape, or choose any card from the deck at random. Place your four chosen cards facedown in a row. When you are ready to begin, turn over all the cards.

FOR EXAMPLE:

ACE *of* SWORDS.

QUEEN *of* CUPS.

THE WORLD.

QUEEN *of* PENTACLES.

4 Look at the major arcana cards. We have one here, the World, so the focus is completion. This major card acts a theme for the reading—a project or goal is about to be achieved. Success and reward are coming.

5 Look at the minor arcana cards. Three suits are shown—Swords, Cups, and Pentacles—so it's likely that the completion the World brings will benefit other areas of your life. Pentacles show money, so you may be paid when you complete the work. Cups reveal emotions, so this project may be close to your heart and bring personal fulfillment. Swords represent thoughts and the intellect, showing that finishing the work or achieving the goal is an expression of your ideas, and now that the work is almost done, you will free up some much-needed mental space.

6 Look at duplicates. There are two Queens. These can represent two aspects of yourself—the Cups, your feelings, and the Coins, the material, worldly aspect. You're in a powerful position financially and in a positive emotional space.

7 Look at the numbers on all four cards. In this example, note how the World's number, XXI, symbolizes the other cards. It has two tens, a repeat number, suggesting the repeat of the two Queens in the reading. The 1 of XXI gives us the Ace of Swords, beginnings. The World, the card of completion, also signifies new beginnings, so you can interpret the Ace as a new start or project that is coming. You might also see the Ace as guidance. To get to your goal, be decisive, put your feelings to one side, and find the most efficient way to tie up loose ends.

1 Look at the major arcana cards and read them together. We have XIII Death and XVII The Star. Death is about endings and letting go, while the Star is a card of hope, creativity, and healing. What links them both is the concept of transformation, so a great change is under way; something may be taken, but this is necessary, and the Star is reassurance that the ending will be more positive than anticipated. Change and transformation are the themes of this reading.

2 Look at the minor arcana card suits, Swords and Wands. Swords, the signifiers of thought and the mind, are accompanied by Wands, suit of desire and drive. This might represent a conflict; you know, intellectually, that you must let go of a situation, but a desire to get your immediate needs met keeps you holding on. Looking at the meaning of the Two of Swords and Four of Wands, we see that the Two of Swords indicates stuckness and procrastination, while the Four of Wands represents freedom and happiness. So the Four can symbolize the release and newfound freedom that comes after Death, but another interpretation is that the Four might represent idealism about the past, which keeps you stuck—with the Two of Swords.

3 The numbers on the cards guide you toward an interpretation. Two and four are numbers of stability but are not dynamic. You may crave stability, but Death has other ideas. The message here is to let go and embrace change.

ANSWERING A QUESTION: **THREE CARDS OR MORE**

Here, we use three cards. The card that represents your question is known as a Significator. In this reading, you choose it deliberately by thinking of your situation and looking at all the cards in the deck to find one that most closely sums it up. You can do this intuitively or see the list below for guidance.

Lay your Significator card faceup and to the left, as shown to the right. Next, take the remaining cards and shuffle them as you think of your question. Choose two cards from the deck at random and place them faceup to the right of the Significator card.

Choosing a Significator	
Work and achievement	Eight of Pentacles
Love	Two of Cups
Debt	Five of Coins
Friendships	Three of Cups
Writing, speaking	Queen of Wands
Travel plans	Two of Wands, Eight of Wands, or VII The Chariot
If someone will contact you	Eight or Page of Wands
About a stuck situation	Two of Swords
Moving house	Knight of Wands
Feeling trapped or restricted	Eight of Swords or XV The Devil
Moving on	Six of Swords or Eight of Cups

FOR EXAMPLE:

Anna asked, "Will this new job/project go well?" She had been offered a new role in her current organization and would be moved to a new department if she accepted the position.

1
Significator

2
Answer

3
Answer

Anna's Significator is the Eight of Pentacles, which signifies work and advancement. The Knight of Swords represents opposition and fear, which Anna interpreted as her potential new manager—he has a reputation for efficiency but is known to be ruthless. The Four of Cups revealed dissatisfaction, due to being managed with a rod of steel, or because, for other reasons, her new role would not prove as stimulating as she had hoped. For confirmation, Anna drew a third card, the Seven of Swords. Traditionally, this means loss; the Knight of Swords might rob Anna of her motivation, shown by the Four of Cups. Overall, the reading presented Anna with the option to refuse the job or to accept that to succeed she would need to be strongly assertive.

Significator

Answer

Answer

Confirmation

PAST, PRESENT, FUTURE

This spread is a tarot classic, and it's one of the most direct methods for getting right to the heart of a question and seeing the potential outcome. You can use this spread to inquire about a specific situation—say, a project, relationship, or finances—or for general insight into the influences most affecting you now.

Shuffle your question or request into the cards, then choose three (from a fan, by cutting the deck, or choosing at random). Lay them out, facedown, in the order shown below. Turn them faceup one at a time or turn them all faceup together—whatever feels right—and begin your interpretation (see the card meanings on pages 136 through 143).

1
Past

2
Present

3
Future

THE **CELTIC CROSS**

The Celtic Cross is the layout that professional readers turn to time and again. It gives more detail and context than the three-card reading, helping you see more aspects of your situation.

Shuffle and choose your cards (see page 118) and then lay the ten cards facedown. Turn over cards 1 to 6 and interpret them in turn, then turn over and interpret cards 7 through 10.

Card 1: Your current situation

Card 2: What is crossing or complementing you

Card 3: The best you can expect at present

Card 4: Hidden factors around you, or the "foundation," the real reason for the reading

Card 5: Past events influencing the present*

Card 6: Your next move*

Card 7: How you see yourself; what you can do

Card 8: Your environment; how others see you

Card 9: Hopes and fears

Card 10: The most likely outcome

*Some readers reverse positions 5 and 6. They lay the central cross, then one card above it and one below, but then lay a card to the right, then a card to the left. You can try the spread in the card order shown below, then try swapping cards 5 and 6 and see how this affects your reading. Go with whatever layout works best for you.

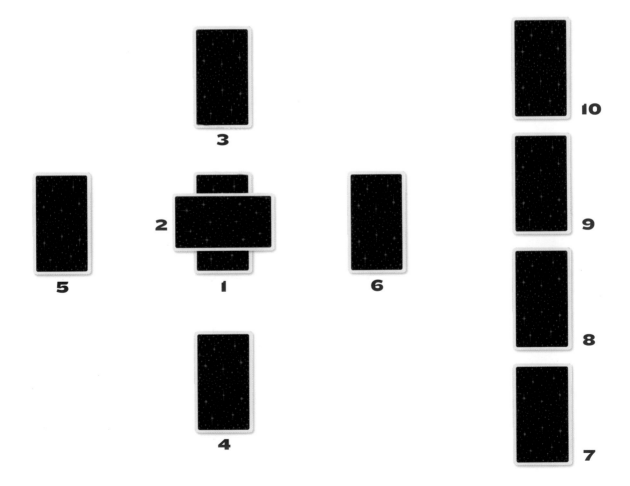

THE WEEK **AHEAD**

To look at the week ahead, shuffle and choose eight cards. First, lay down the Significator card facedown, followed by seven further cards in the order shown below. This order comes from the planets associated with the days of the week and the speed of their orbits according to the Greek scholar Ptolemy (90–168 CE). For example, Monday, or Moon day, is first because its orbit is fastest, followed by Mercury (Wednesday), then Venus (Friday), and so on.

Keep the Significator facedown, but turn all the other cards faceup and interpret them. Finally, turn over the Significator; this gives you the overall theme of the week and helps you bring together the meanings of the other cards.

Significator: the general theme of the week

1 Monday

2 Wednesday

3 Friday

4 Sunday

5 Tuesday

6 Thursday

7 Saturday

Significator

| **1** | **5** | **2** | **6** | **3** | **7** | **4** |
| MON | TUE | WED | THUR | FRI | SAT | SUN |

THE **WHOLE-PICTURE** SPREAD

This is a great spread to try when you're procrastinating or when you have that feeling there's something you need to see or understand, but you can't quite sense what it is. It's also helpful when you need to problem-solve or crave inspiration because the cards can show what you might be missing; perhaps a new angle of inquiry that helps you move forward.

Shuffle and choose your cards (see page 118). Lay out cards 1 through 10 facedown, turn over all the cards apart from 9 and 10, and begin your interpretation. Finally, turn over 9 and 10, which reveal what might be missing and what you might do.

1 You/your situation

2 Intuition: What feels right

3 Experience: Your strengths

4 Ambition or goal: What approach to take

5 Joys

6 Sorrows

7 Potential gain

8 Outcome

9 What's missing? What do I need to see?

10 What action can I take now?

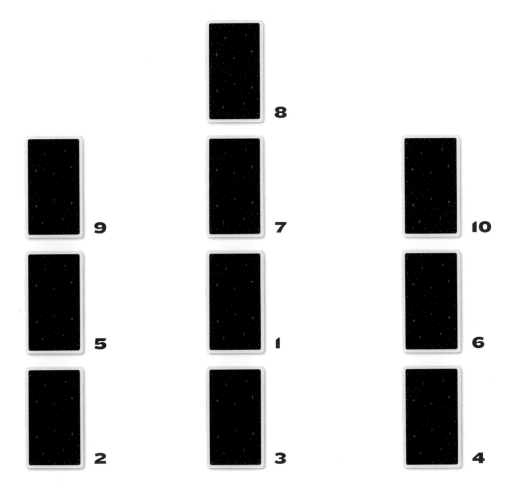

CLEANSING YOUR DECK
BETWEEN READINGS

Cards absorb the energies of their environment and hold the emotion of a reading. So, before you read, you'll need to clear down your deck. This does not delete your connection with your cards; the cleansing ritual releases any old energy that might affect the next reading. It's tarot housekeeping.

Go through the deck and turn any reversed (upside-down cards) the right way up.

Next, choose one or both of these instant cleansing techniques:

Blowing: Hold your deck in one hand and flick it as you blow across it.

Knocking: Hold the deck in one hand, with the cards facedown, and knock out unwanted energies with a firm, single knock on the top of the deck.

CARD MEANINGS

The interpretations for the cards appear here, but also note your intuitive responses to your cards; it's worth taking a note of your own impressions first, before reading the traditional card meanings here, which are for guidance rather than rote learning. Many readers do not use set meanings—they interpret according to their response to the symbols and card colors and are guided by their intuition—so be free to work in a way that feels right for you.

WHAT IF TWO PEOPLE GET THE SAME OR SIMILAR CARDS?

If a deck is not cleared down between readings, the cards may repeat in your next reading. If this happens, ask the querent to shuffle the deck again. If the cards are the same as the first layout, go with them for the reading.

FINDING THE QUINTESSENCE

Add up the numbers of the cards in your reading, reduce it to a number between 1 and 21, and you have the number of a major arcana card. This card gives you additional guidance or advice at the end of your reading.

Add up the numbers of the "pip" cards—those numbered Ace through Ten, where Ace is 1—plus the numbers of the major arcana cards. Ignore the Court cards. So, for example, if you had the Ace of Wands, Six of Cups, the Hierophant, and the Hanged Man in a reading, you would add up: 1 (Ace), 6, 5 (V The Hierophant) and 12 (XII The Hanged Man). So: $1 + 6 + 5 + 12 = 24$. As this is more than 21, add the digits together: $2 + 4 = 6$. This is the number of VI The Lovers, which signifies an important decision.

You can use this technique at the end of every reading, regardless of the number of cards used in a spread.

The Major Arcana

0 THE FOOL

Keywords: Innocence, risk, beginnings.

The Fool marks the beginning of the tarot's major arcana cycle and so represents a major new life chapter. This is your call to adventure, to journey into unknown territory through physical travel or a new career or spiritual path; this adventure is not without risk, however. The cliffs represent danger; the mountains represent challenges; and the dog, barking a warning at our Fool, is a reminder to look before he leaps. The card can often appear in a reading after a relationship breakup as a sign of awakening to new possibilities ahead.

Advice: Embrace adventure but know the risks.

Reversed meaning: Idealistic thinking may cloud practical considerations; foolishness.

I THE MAGICIAN

Keywords: Action, willpower, success.

The Magician is the tarot's manifestor, transforming thought into action through his will; he understands the flow of energy, symbolized by the figure eight or lemniscate, and works with it to create powerful change. The Magician calls you to create and communicate, and the card often heralds new projects, travel, and news. You have the resources you need to act, shown by the four minor arcana suit symbols on the Magician's table: intelligence and reason (the Sword), heart (Cup), security and finance (Pentacle), and drive and passion (Wand).

Advice: Manifest your ideas now.

Reversed meaning: Deception; being charmed by an untrustworthy individual; also, miscommunication and delays to plans.

THE HIGH PRIESTESS.

THE EMPRESS.

II THE HIGH PRIESTESS

Keywords: Secrets, wisdom, the spiritual world.

The High Priestess is the clairvoyant, the translator between the realm of spirit and the earth plane. She asks you to connect with your intuition and to follow your spiritual calling. The card also denotes the need for privacy and keeping secrets and highlights the importance of the inner world and the power of unconscious knowing. The High Priestess as a keeper of wisdom arises too for learning and mentoring and the teacher or spirit guide who connects with you when the time is right.

Advice: Value privacy and your spiritual practice.

Reversed meaning: Following a wrong path or breaking a confidence; a person who uses secret knowledge to gain power or status.

III THE EMPRESS

Keywords: Abundance, generosity, creativity.

The Empress brings abundance, so finances, relationships, and domestic projects thrive now. Harmony and balance benefit you, so this is a card of reassurance if you have been struggling financially or wondering if a relationship will grow. The Empress also denotes generosity and the ability to give and receive loving support. As the earth goddess, she connects us with the cycles of nature, family, and fertility. You may also seed ideas for new creative projects.

Advice: Nurture people and projects.

Reversed meaning: Financial challenges or fertility issues, creative blocks, or relationships out of balance.

IV THE EMPEROR

Keywords: Control, security, order, authority, ambition.

The Emperor is the father or traditional male partner, a figure of authority and leadership. In a reading, he shows order is restored, and you are back in control of a situation. As the Emperor protects the boundaries of his territory, the card calls you to prioritize what is important to you and to take a methodical rather than intuitive approach; following due process gives the best results. As he represents authority, an additional meaning is taking on more responsibility and power; the card often arises in readings to show promotion.

Advice: Put practical matters first; get organized.

Reversed meaning: Feeling restricted by outdated attitudes or bullied by a domineering yet ineffectual individual.

V THE HIEROPHANT

Keywords: Education, unity, spiritual direction. The Hierophant denotes unity, but he holds many diverse meanings: education, orthodox beliefs, commitment, and public life. Overall, though, when he appears in a reading, you're about to move up a level; you honor your personal growth by being willing to learn and accept new responsibility, so you may embark on an educational course, take on a community role that may involve mediation, or decide to take a business or creative venture to new heights. Spiritually, the card shows self-connection, wisdom, and divine law. In relationships, the Hierophant brings a love commitment such as marriage.

Advice: Commit and learn.

Reversed meaning: The potential abuse of power; unfair criticism.

VI THE LOVERS

Keywords: Love and relationships, maturity, decisions.

The Lovers foretell an important decision. You may need to decide to stay part of a couple or be single; to choose between potential partners; or between lust or long-time love (a traditional association of the card is love triangles). Although the card highlights love and relationships, it has meaning in every reading. In work and business, for example, you may have the option of short-term contracts or permanent work. The best decision may not be the easiest, but the Lovers ask you to look beyond immediate gratification toward long-term happiness and fulfillment.

Advice: Take the path that supports your future growth.

Reversed meaning: Being let down in a relationship or taking the easiest, but not necessarily the best, option.

VII THE CHARIOT

Keywords: Determination, victory, a journey.

The Chariot shows you are moving into a success phase. The charioteer directs his sphinx-chariot by willpower rather than harness, so steady determination moves him forward; he cannot allow his ego to get out of control. The light and dark sphinxes symbolize the dark and light aspects of his personality and the stars symbolize cosmic protection. In a reading, the card says that if you take careful responsibility for your career and personal life, you will continue to progress and grow. It can also predict significant journeys, a new vehicle, new work and residences, and/or a commitment to be fully in a relationship—or alone.

Advice: Your determination brings success.

Reversed meaning: Arrogance and displays of ego; important details may be overlooked; journeys may be delayed.

VIII STRENGTH

Keywords: Patience, tension, strength.

The maiden symbolizes the higher self and the lion symbolizes our baser instincts. Holding open the animal's jaws, she is peaceful and patient, holding her ground. The lemniscate signifies the flow of life and infinite possibility. In a reading, Strength says you may need your inner strength when dealing with conflict within yourself or with an external challenge to your position. The need for compassion is an additional meaning, and Strength also appears in readings to show physical strength and recovery after illness or stress.

Advice: Call upon your inner strength.

Reversed meaning: Avoiding conflict rather than confronting a challenge.

IX THE HERMIT

Keywords: Solitude, healing, contemplation.

The Hermit, guided only by the light of his lamp, travels alone in darkness. This is the card of contemplation and shows a time for solitude; this is a choice, rather than a situation to be endured, however. You may need time to write, study, meditate, or heal, or you may need peace and time away from pressure. You may feel called to reflect on a recent event and more deeply understand your role within it. The card often shows up after a relationship breakup or to illuminate a new educational or spiritual path.

Advice: Look within for the wisdom you seek.

Reversed meaning: Unwanted solitude; you may be feeling unsupported or rejected, but this situation can and will change.

WHEEL *of* FORTUNE.

JUSTICE.

X THE WHEEL OF FORTUNE

Keywords: Fate, improvement, intuition.

The Wheel represents Fate, the working of destiny in the world. As it turns, good fortune comes, so this is a card of hope and optimism. Problems are solved, and you move to a happier, productive phase. As the card is linked with fate, it suggests a connection with other realms and can show psychic ability, especially if it appears with card II, The High Priestess. As XIII Death takes away what is no longer needed, the Wheel gives you the gift of luck and great potential for achievement.

Advice: Allow and appreciate destined gifts.

Reversed meaning: Even when reversed, the outlook is positive. A difficult phase is almost over; an upturn is coming.

XI JUSTICE

Keywords: Balance, perception, objectivity.

The Justice card reveals being judged by others, rather than the self. In a reading, the card signifies the law profession, along with assessment and decisions in other life areas. And justice will be done, provided you are deserving and speak the truth. Past errors are put right, so if you have been mistreated or your reputation damaged, the card is reassurance that the situation will be positively resolved. Life comes back into balance.

Advice: Stay true to your values.

Reversed meaning: There may be unfair treatment, discrimination, or a miscarriage of justice.

THE HANGED MAN.

DEATH.

XII THE HANGED MAN

Keywords: Waiting, sacrifice, enlightenment.

The Hanged Man is often linked with Norse god Odin, who hung from the world tree, after which he was given the gift of prophecy. His time of suspension between worlds—a shamanic initiation—was worthwhile because of the magical gift he received. In a reading, this card shows you in limbo, waiting for a decision, for events to unfold. Use this time to see your situation from another angle; there may be a higher purpose to this stasis, an insight that awaits you. The card can also show that you may need to make a sacrifice to move forward.

Advice: See your situation from another perspective.

Reversed meaning: Naïveté; making unnecessary sacrifices.

XIII DEATH

Keywords: Endings, release, transformation.

Death is not physical death, but a process of change through which our lives are transformed for the better. We may not welcome this skeletal figure with his scythe, but he is a representation of the cycles of change that is necessary and absolute. It is time to accept what cannot be part of the future. In a reading, the card often arises to show the end of a relationship, job, or old situation. With Death comes truth—down to the bone, you now see what remains. Endings bring beginnings, so this card in your reading also signals new beginnings and growth.

Advice: Let go without fear.

Reversed meaning: Resistance to moving forward; holding on to the past.

XIV TEMPERANCE

Keywords: Balance, reconciliation, healing, angelic guidance.

The Temperance angel pours water between two pitchers; the water flows in two directions, so we are witnessing a miracle. You too may need a little divine intervention to deal with current pressures and demands, to find the right formula to keep everything flowing. Temperance signifies the need to carefully negotiate terms and often to mediate between difficult people. Relationships need emotional balance, and in financial affairs, the card often asks us to temper, or control, spending. Spiritually, Temperance suggests angelic guidance.

Advice: Get the balance right and you can succeed.

Reversed meaning: Being a martyr to others' unreasonable demands; being emotionally overwhelmed; overspending and debt.

XV THE DEVIL

Keywords: Enslavement, temptation, contracts.

The Devil, the shadow side of card VI The Lovers, symbolizes temptation and agreements that are, or have become, restrictive. These may be unhealthy contracts we have with ourselves or other binds that enslave us. The card also reveals toxic relationships, lust, addiction issues, and negative thinking patterns—whatever seeks to control you. As the two figures on the card are not chained to the Devil, they can walk free whenever they choose. You, too, can free yourself from any negative situation more easily than you think.

Advice: You can be free now.

Reversed meaning: The restriction of the upright card may feel acute, but you can break the ties that do not serve you.

XVI THE TOWER

Keywords: Destruction, enlightenment.

The Tower signifies sudden destruction: The Tower falls and two people are cast out. In a flash, you see the truth of a situation; what you had thought was secure is subject to greater forces. There is no reason or blame for it. In this way, the Tower is a card of enlightenment and breakthrough, bringing release after an intense buildup. The card appears in readings to show the sudden ending of a relationship, issues with a house, or a huge knock to the ego. The impact may be shocking, but you are now able to rebuild.

Advice: Surrender and welcome the new.

Reversed meaning: The Tower may leave you reeling, but there is no need for bitterness or blame. It's time to recover.

XVII THE STAR

Keywords: Hope, guidance, inspiration, creativity.

The Star maiden pours water from the pitcher of the past, to her left, and the pitcher of the present; the water symbolizes flowing thought and emotion. She nurtures the pool of life, guided by the star above her. The twilight denotes the magical time between night and day, signifying transition; changes are coming that will lead you closer to your higher purpose. In a reading, the Star also brings creative opportunities and divine guidance. The card is also associated with healing, as her watering gives nourishment and leads to growth.

Advice: Be hopeful and inspired.

Reversed meaning: When feeling unsupported, don't give up; follow the guiding light within.

XVIII THE MOON

Keywords: Illusion, dreams, crisis.

The Moon is the card of dreams, mystery, intuition, and doubt. In moonlight, nothing is as it seems, and the crayfish, symbol of the soul, must decide to go forward and escape the dog and wolf or stay safely in the water. The crayfish can signify a realization that is just under the surface of your conscious awareness, so this card is often a sign of disturbance—something important needs your attention. However, this is not a matter of applying logic. Your dreams and creative or spiritual practices may help you see what is at stake.

Advice: Let your intuition guide you toward a realization or decision.

Reversed meaning: Avoiding a deep or complex issue.

XIX THE SUN

Keywords: Success, protection, health, happiness.

The Sun is one of the most positive cards in the tarot deck, as it denotes happiness, achievement, and recuperation; stress dissolves as you enjoy simple pleasures, from spending time with family to enjoying restorative time alone—however you like to recharge. The sunflowers represent growth and health, and the wall represents protection, so the Sun can also indicate recovery after illness and, more generally, vitality and reward. At a literal level, the card sees you on vacation away from home or enjoying creative pursuits that nurture your inner child. The Sun overrules any negative cards close by it in a spread.

Advice: Relax; appreciate your blessings.

Reversed meaning: There is no specific negative meaning for the optimistic Sun, other than potential delay to plans.

XX JUDGMENT

Keywords: Assessment, second chances, forgiveness, awakening.

With Judgment, we judge ourselves, whereas XI Justice judges us. Judgment brings a turning point and an opportunity to revisit the past in order to move on. The angel symbolizes awakening or seeing an old situation in a new light. As memories resurface, you may decide to give a relationship or other past situation a second chance; this may be due to a new spirit of forgiveness or the broader perspective that time and distance bring. An additional meaning of the card is spiritual connection and receiving messages from guides and loved ones in spirit.

Advice: Look back with compassion.

Reversed meaning: Judging yourself too harshly or living in the past; holding on to feelings of regret or shame that could be released.

XXI THE WORLD

Keywords: Completion, success, reward, joy.

The World, the last card in the tarot's major arcana sequence, draws us to a conclusion before the cycle begins again with 0 The Fool. It marks the successful completion and celebration of a life phase or goal; you have come full circle and are rewarded for achievement in your professional life and relationships. You may also see your horizons expand, with a broader perspective on life or an opportunity to travel to a new destination. The World also suggests togetherness within the self and others; you are at one with the world.

Advice: Enjoy your deserved success.

Reversed meaning: There is no negative meaning for this joyful card, only that completion and reward may be delayed for a time.

The Minor Arcana: Cups

ACE OF CUPS

Upright meaning: New love and new passions; overflowing emotion; joy and blessings; also, fertility, pregnancy, and the birth of a baby or project.

Reversed meaning: Feeling overwhelmed; worries about relationships; fertility issues.

TWO OF CUPS

Upright meaning: Love and peace; happy professional and love partnerships; meeting a soul mate or kindred spirit.

Reversed meaning: Trust issues; imbalance or disappointment in a partnership.

THREE OF CUPS

Upright meaning: Celebrations, friendship, and flirtation; thriving creatively and emotionally.

Reversed meaning: Feeling distanced from support networks; the need to take extra care of yourself.

FOUR OF CUPS

Upright meaning: A plateau; feeling bored or flat; a need to see the good opportunities on offer.

Reversed meaning: Stubbornness, cynicism, or deeper boredom; the need for action.

FIVE OF CUPS

Upright meaning: Loss and sadness; however, there are still some avenues to explore; stay positive.

Reversed meaning: A period of sadness or instability is ending; look forward to better times ahead.

SIX OF CUPS

Upright meaning: A visitor arrives, often a person from the past, bringing happy reminiscences.

Reversed meaning: Nostalgia that becomes a refuge rather than a temporary pleasure.

SEVEN OF CUPS

Upright meaning: Dreams and possibilities that are not yet manifest; there is much potential, but everything feels up in the air.

Reversed meaning: The need to wait for information before making a choice.

EIGHT OF CUPS

Upright meaning: It's time to leave an old situation behind; go your own way.

Reversed meaning: Feeling abandoned or neglected; poor timing.

NINE OF CUPS

Upright meaning: Joy and sharing as wishes come true; love, generosity, and relationship happiness.

Reversed meaning: Fixating on a goal that may not be important; alternatively, dealing with others' egos.

TEN OF CUPS

Upright meaning: Relationship and family happiness; also, a new home or dream come true.

Reversed meaning: Pressure to conform to others' expectations; there's no need.

PAGE OF CUPS

Upright meaning: A new friend, love, or idea; creativity, dreaminess, imagination, and fun.

Reversed meaning: Relationship issues; misunderstandings and oversensitivity to criticism.

KNIGHT OF CUPS

Upright meaning: Romance and opportunity; can indicate new friendships, a proposal, or offer.

Reversed meaning: Idealism without foundation; empty promises or commitment issues.

QUEEN OF CUPS

Upright meaning: Love and happiness are important to you now; this is a good time for creative projects and overall, following your intuition and your heart.

Reversed meaning: Emotional or financial pressure; demanding or jealous behavior.

KING OF CUPS

Upright meaning: Support and love; being open-hearted in the way you communicate; empathy can resolve differences.

Reversed meaning: Vulnerability and defensiveness; dealing with volatile behavior.

The Minor Arcana: Pentacles

ACE OF PENTACLES

Upright meaning: A new beginning, such as a new job, business, or home; brightens any negative minor arcana cards that fall close to it in a spread.

Reversed meaning: Financial problems, such as debt or cash flow; also materialism.

TWO OF PENTACLES

Upright meaning: Weighing up options; deciding how to manage money and a choice between locations, jobs, or courses.

Reversed meaning: Imbalance in a partnership; commitment or financial issues need careful consideration.

THREE OF PENTACLES

Upright meaning: Being appreciated for your work; early success in a venture or project; also, job interviews, talks, and presentations.

Reversed meaning: Unfinished business; frustration and delay.

FOUR OF PENTACLES

Upright meaning: Being financially secure; putting down roots and finding balance; financial challenges are over.

Reversed meaning: Becoming too entrenched in routine; clinging to material possessions.

FIVE OF PENTACLES

Upright meaning: Loss or isolation, which may be financial or social; however, the card usually reveals fear of losing something, rather than reality.

Reversed meaning: Hardship that challenges you; look for support, as you may have more resources than you think.

SIX OF PENTACLES

Upright meaning: Money is given to you; it may be a gift, bonus, or other reward. Equally, you may be the giver, generously supporting others.

Reversed meaning: Your kindness is not repaid yet, or money due to you is outstanding.

SEVEN OF PENTACLES

Upright meaning: The need for continued effort—this situation has great potential, so stay focused on the goal rather than doubting your path.

Reversed meaning: Doubt or disillusion; walking away too quickly from a potentially good opportunity.

EIGHT OF PENTACLES

Upright meaning: Hard work, perfectionism, and professionalism; solid achievement and reward, plus further development opportunities.

Reversed meaning: Feeling overworked and underpaid or otherwise unappreciated.

NINE OF PENTACLES

Upright meaning: Security and contentment; proud of your achievements, you may give yourself a reward and enjoy some luxury and/or leisure time.

Reversed meaning: Materialism, or dealing with overspending; financial insecurity.

TEN OF PENTACLES

Upright meaning: Prosperity and family; the happy joining of two families through marriage; generosity, love, and support.

Reversed meaning: Miscommunication between generations of a family; issues around money or inheritance.

PAGE OF PENTACLES

Upright meaning: A financial offer, such as new work or a new venture, with opportunities to develop your skills.

Reversed meaning: Financial or property issues; meanness; lack of flexibility.

KNIGHT OF PENTACLES

Upright meaning: Good financial planning and reward for hard work; also, loyalty and honesty.

Reversed meaning: Potential dishonesty; the need to take control of finances, seek trustworthy advice, and check agreements.

QUEEN OF PENTACLES

Upright meaning: Generosity and wisdom; solid friendship, comfort, and support; good health and financial security.

Reversed meaning: Financial problems—overspending or meanness, or waiting for money owed to be paid.

KING OF PENTACLES

Upright meaning: Money and security; trust, generosity, and practical support; problems are solved.

Reversed meaning: Greed and materialism; selfishness and, at worst, fraudulent activity.

The Minor Arcana: Swords

ACE OF SWORDS

Upright meaning: A breakthrough or decision that brings success; clear thinking and insight; the card brightens any negative minor arcana cards that appear close to it.

Reversed meaning: A decision goes against you; feeling dominated or outwitted.

TWO OF SWORDS

Upright meaning: Procrastination or a truce; time to reflect on an upcoming decision; a need to move forward.

Reversed meaning: Feeling stuck; not having the information or confidence to make a positive choice.

THREE OF SWORDS

Upright meaning: Upset and sorrow, which can be due to a third party in a relationship or in your professional life.

Reversed meaning: Knowing the truth; releasing emotions to move on.

FOUR OF SWORDS

Upright meaning: Time out to recover from stress or illness; taking refuge; in love, a relationship goes on hold.

Reversed meaning: An unwelcome interruption to your routine; the need to accept the situation.

FIVE OF SWORDS

Upright meaning: An unwinnable battle; feeling defeated; a time to pick yourself up and look forward.

Reversed meaning: Feeling humiliated or bullied by a domineering individual.

SIX OF SWORDS

Upright meaning: Moving on from problems to peace; a time of unrest is over; you may also travel at this time.

Reversed meaning: You can make progress but may need to let go of an attitude or problem first.

SEVEN OF SWORDS

Upright meaning: Insecurity; you may need to protect what is yours and be aware of any dishonest behavior.

Reversed meaning: Feeling like a victim; there is a danger you may surrender to circumstances rather than hold your position.

EIGHT OF SWORDS

Upright meaning: Feeling hemmed in by your thoughts; overthinking and restriction may be the cause, but you can think your way out.

Reversed meaning: Strong emotions such as fear or guilt may make you feel frustrated or oppressed; this too will pass.

NINE OF SWORDS

Upright meaning: Anxiety and stress disturb your peace; try to let go of any underlying fear and trust that the situation will improve.

Reversed meaning: Feeling alone; ask for support, as you do not have to suffer in silence.

TEN OF SWORDS

Upright meaning: A swift and sudden ending; this may be unexpected, but you can now move on.

Reversed meaning: A need to cling to the past; try to accept things as they are now.

PAGE OF SWORDS

Upright meaning: Agreements and contracts; the need to pay close attention to detail and have your wits about you.

Reversed meaning: Sniping and underhandedness; tactlessness.

KNIGHT OF SWORDS

Upright meaning: Unpredictability, opposition, and conflict; the need for calm resolution.

Reversed meaning: Mind games and drama; a battle that is best abandoned.

QUEEN OF SWORDS

Upright meaning: Independence, intelligence, and strength; often, a single woman with great strength of character.

Reversed meaning: Obsessiveness and unfair treatment; ruthless attitudes.

KING OF SWORDS

Upright meaning: Ambition and decisions, which may be legal or official; being judged; taking strong, swift action.

Reversed meaning: Being overruled or dominated by a headstrong opponent.

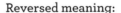

The Minor Arcana: Wands

ACE OF WANDS

Upright meaning: Good news and beginnings; inspiration, movement, and travel; fertile ideas and children.

Reversed meaning: Miscommunication and delay; potential fertility issues.

TWO OF WANDS

Upright meaning: A new partnership; plans take shape; travel or new creative ideas beckon.

Reversed meaning: Delays to plans and potential doubt concerning love or professional partnerships.

THREE OF WANDS

Upright meaning: Travel, success, and potentially new love; creativity and self-expression.

Reversed meaning: The need for patience; delays may frustrate you, but success is coming.

FOUR OF WANDS

Upright meaning: Feeling happy and free; the card can show the return to childhood haunts, a new relationship, and the honeymoon phase.

Reversed meaning: Delays may affect your plans; these may be frustrating, but they are temporary.

FIVE OF WANDS

Upright meaning: Competitions and tests; the need to stand your ground and make sure you are heard.

Reversed meaning: A need for discretion; you may be surrounded by people who are untrustworthy, or being casual with the truth.

SIX OF WANDS

Upright meaning: Success and validation, particularly in tests, examinations, and personal projects.

Reversed meaning: Victory is coming; your reward may be delayed, but keep up the effort.

SEVEN OF WANDS

Upright meaning: Standing your ground; stay true to your values and purpose, and you will succeed.

Reversed meaning: Feeling locked in an ongoing dispute, or having to continually defend yourself.

EIGHT OF WANDS

Upright meaning: Events speed up, with news, communication, and travel; stuck situations take a leap forward; also, good news concerning relationships.

Reversed meaning: Frustration due to delays and misunderstanding or lack of communication.

NINE OF WANDS

Upright meaning: Strength, but also overvigilance; being wary of opposition; you may need to let go a little to free up ideas and energy.

Reversed meaning: Becoming defensive because you have had to be strong for a long time.

TEN OF WANDS

Upright meaning: Losing perspective; you may be overloaded with responsibility just now; it's time to prioritize rather than agree to every demand.

Reversed meaning: Pressure; feeling habitually overwhelmed; it is time to step back.

PAGE OF WANDS

Upright meaning: Good news, particularly concerning projects and new ideas; assess each offer before you commit; also, can predict a happy reunion.

Reversed meaning: Confusion and miscommunication; being distracted, or not being heard.

KNIGHT OF WANDS

Upright meaning: Making progress; stuck issues get resolved and a romance may begin; can also reveal moving home.

Reversed meaning: Plans may be put on hold, leading to frustration; also, someone may be unclear as to their goals, or even insincere.

QUEEN OF WANDS

Upright meaning: Dynamic self-expression; a great time to get projects under way and communicate ideas.

Reversed meaning: Creative block, or other temporary delays to plans and projects.

KING OF WANDS

Upright meaning: Confidence and leadership; being open to new people, ideas, and experiences and being the initiator.

Reversed meaning: Overconfidence; a lack of listening and sharing; feeling silenced or unable to express yourself.

6 NUMEROLOGY

THE ART OF NUMBER INTERPRETATION

Numerology is the art of number interpretation. Numbers are believed to have unique energetic signatures, which have meaning—and these meanings reveal much about your future potential and character. The numbers used in numerology are calculated from your name and date of birth. You can progress to adding up other numbers that are connected to you, such as your house, apartment, or cell phone number. In this chapter, you'll see how to calculate your numbers, and you'll discover how to use this knowledge in key life areas or goals.

UNDER-STANDING NUMEROLOGY

Modern numerology has a trifold ancestry: Pythagorean numerology, kabbalic numerology, and Chaldean numerology, a relative of the kabbalic system. The most popular method is that of Greek philosopher and mathematician Pythagoras (c. 570–c. 495 BCE).

Known today for his theorem on right-angle triangles, Pythagoras perceived the universe as a series of mathematical relationships. Numbers 1 through 10 (rather than 1 through 9, as in contemporary numerology) were considered essential numbers in Pythagorean thinking. The importance of 10 is echoed, too, in the ten sephirots, or spheres of consciousness on the Tree of Life in kabbala, the Jewish mystical system. Sefer Yetzirah, a kabbalistic text written in the second century CE, presented gematria—the assignation of each letter of the Hebrew alphabet with a numerical value to interpret Hebrew scriptures.

Today, we are more number-aware than we might realize: Many of us have lucky numbers and hold with old number superstitions. Thirteen is considered unlucky; however, in Italy, 13 is considered lucky. Chinese numerology holds that the numbers 168 and 888 bring good fortune and success, while 4 is considered unlucky. As a result, fourth floor numbering in some high-rise hotels in Asia is skipped. While beliefs around numbers vary from culture to culture, at heart we all have a personal response to numbers at a conscious or intuitive level.

NUMEROLOGY IN OTHER ARTS

Numerology is deeply embedded in other divinatory arts, from astrology to the I Ching and tarot. In tarot reading, the numbers of the major arcana cards in a spread can be added up and reduced to a single number, which relates to another major card, giving an additional layer of meaning to the reading. In Western occult tradition, planets are linked with a series of numbers expressed as magic squares, while feng shui uses the Lo Shu or ancient magic square to assess the chi or energy of space.

THE CYCLES OF 9

In modern numerology, we primarily use the numbers 1 through 9, the nine single digits, each of which has a unique vibration. These nine numbers express nine potential aspects of the self, contained within a journey. The journey begins with 1, the individual, and ends at 9, the greatest manifestation of our possible contribution to humanity. A new cycle begins with 10, as 10 (1 + 0) reduces to 1, the beginning. We can see this cycle as:

1 Innovation: The individual

2 Cooperation: Partnership

3 Self-expression: Creativity

4 Order: Establishment

5 Expansion: Adventure

6 Love and protection: Community

7 Mystery and intellect: Wisdom

8 Material success: Power

9 Spirituality and courage: Global vision

Numbers 11 and 22 are known as master numbers and are included as key numbers alongside 1 through 9. It is believed that these numbers have an intense vibration: They may mean you have a deep calling and the potential to make a significant contribution, although certain sacrifices may be needed along the way.

So, in total, there are 11 number profiles given (see page 186), but you have more than one number. Numerology gives you a way to calculate a whole series of numbers that reflect your inner and outer selves and to help you to divine your future prospects.

HOW TO **CALCULATE YOUR NUMBERS**

All you need is your date of birth and your name, from which you can calculate your Life Path number, Destiny number, Soul number, and Personality numbers; it's a matter of adding together the numbers in your birth date, reducing them to a single digit (or in some cases, including 11 and 22), and looking up the numbers equivalent to the letters in your name. We use the whole name to calculate the Destiny number, only the consonants for the Personality numbers, and just the vowels for the Soul number—so your name alone holds a set of key numbers that unlock a meaning just for you.

Your Life Path Number: Life Direction

Your Life Path number is the sum of all the numbers in your date of birth, reduced to 1–9, 11, or 22. It reveals your life direction, showing how you might progress.

FOR EXAMPLE:

Date of birth: October 29, 1976

$1 + 0 + 2 + 9 + 1 + 9 + 7 + 6 = 35$

$3 + 5 = 8$

So, the Life Path number for this person is 8.

Also, take note of any repeating numbers in the date of birth. In this example, we have:

1 0 2 9 1 9 7 6

There are two number 9s, so 9 would be a secondary Life Path number, with 8 being the dominant number. In this case, you would look up both 8 and 9 in the number interpretations on pages 186 through 191.

Your Destiny Number: Life Lessons

Your Destiny number is the sum of numbers equivalent to your full name on your birth certificate, reduced to 1–9, 11, or 22. This number tells you about the lessons you learn throughout life. See the chart below to work out how all the letters in your name translate into numbers.

1	2	3	4	5	6	7	8	9
A	B	C	D	E	F	G	H	I
J	K	L	M	N	O	P	Q	R
S	T	U	V	W	X	Y	Z	

EXAMPLE:

Full name: PAUL DAVID MASON

PAUL = 7 + 1 + 3 + 3 = 14; 1 + 4 = 5

DAVID = 4 + 1 + 4 + 9 + 4 = 22; 2 + 2 = 4

MASON = 4 + 1 + 1 + 6 + 5 = 17; 1 + 7 = 8

5 + 4 + 8 = 17

1 + 7 = 8

Therefore, Paul's Destiny number is 8.

Your Soul Number: Your Deeper Self

Your Soul Number is the sum of numbers equivalent to the vowels in your full name on your birth certificate, reduced to 1–9, 11, or 22. The Soul number signifies your deeper self and your intuitive desires.

EXAMPLE:

Full name: LAUREN TATE

LAUREN = 1 + 3 + 5 = 9 (counting only the vowels A, U, and E)

TATE = 1 + 5 = 6

9 + 6 = 15

1 + 5 = 6

So, Lauren's Soul number is 6.

Note that W and Y also count as vowels, but only in certain instances.

Y is a vowel when it is sounded as an I, such as in Bryn, and when it comes after a vowel and informs that vowel's sound, such as in Hayford (the y makes the long "a" sound).

W is a vowel when it comes after a vowel and informs that vowel's sound, as in Jewell or Howard.

Your Personality Numbers: Facets of Your Personality

Personality numbers are calculated by adding up numbers equivalent to the consonants in your full name, acquired name(s), and nickname(s). These numbers reflect the different faces you show to the world—at work and in personal relationships, for example. Add together the consonants' numbers for each name and write them down.

At work, Samantha is a 2; with friends and family, a 5; and in her freelance photography work, an 8. One interpretation would be that in her day job, Samantha's success depends upon cooperation and strong working partnerships (2), while her freelance business is a platform for great future achievement (8). As a 5 with friends and family, she shows the freedom-loving side of her personality, enjoying trips away, connecting easily with others, and being willing to take risks.

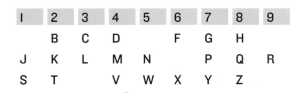

1	2	3	4	5	6	7	8	9
	B	C	D		F	G	H	
J	K	L	M	N		P	Q	R
S	T		V	W	X	Y	Z	

EXAMPLE:

Work name: Samantha

1 + 4 + 5 + 2 + 8 = 20 (counting only the consonants S, M, N, T and H)

2 + 0 = 2

Friends and family name: Sam

1 + 4 = 5

Name used for freelance photography business: Samantha Fry

1 + 4 + 5 + 2 + 8 + 6 + 9 = 35

3 + 5 = 8

Note that the Y in Fry counts as a vowel, so we only include the F and R in the surname.

Each number from 1 to 9 is aligned, where known, with a symbol, day of the week, color, and crystal. The numbers also have astrological correspondences, with a star (the Sun), astronomical body (the Moon), or a planet. Numerologists disagree about some planetary and number associations, in which case several planets may be listed. You will also see best dates of the month if that number is your Life Path number. For example, if you have a Life Path number of 1, the best days for you are the 1st, 10th, 19th, and 28th. (The 19th adds up to 10; 1 + 0 = 1.) These days are those most auspicious for you because their energetic vibration aligns with 1 as your Life Path.

THE NUMBER 0

Zero expresses both nothing and all the other numbers; associated with Pluto, the planet of darkness and the unknown, zero symbolizes infinite possibility. It cannot come up as one of your personal numbers, but it is worth noting if it appears in your date of birth. For example, if you were born on 10/10/2000, you would have five zeros, more than any number. This may indicate you have an all-or-nothing attitude and strong views. Also, given that nothing, or zero, is the goal of Zen, you may have a spiritual or philosophical nature.

Number 1: The Monad—Innovation

One represents light and the primal aspect of God or Source, symbolized by a dot within a circle, a concept attributed to the Pythagoreans. One is the number of unity, deity, and divine intelligence. One denotes oneness with the divine, singularity, action, beginnings, and opportunities. Ones are believed to be highly individual character types.

Symbol: A dot in the center of a circle

Star: The Sun

Day: Sunday

Color: Orange

Crystal: Ruby

Best days of the month for 1 as Life Path: 1st, 10th, 19th, 28th

Character influences: Ones are tenacious, focused, and single-minded. You can achieve great things because you are motivated to make things happen your way. You do not rely on others to fulfill all your needs, and you are willing to step out alone, which means taking certain risks. You may be a visionary entrepreneur, a leader, or simply someone who wishes to live in a way that suits you, regardless of pressure to conform. Because you have such a strong sense of self, others lean on you. Although you do not invite attention or seek power, you support others and will take on huge responsibility if the situation requires it. One also symbolizes divinity and Oneness with the universe. You nurture your own relationship with spirit.

Shadow character: Intolerance and stubbornness; disinterest in others' opinions or advice; arrogance.

Advice: Have courage; go your own way.

Number 2: The Duad—
Empathy and Cooperation

Two is the number of equality and unity in diversity. Diversity encompasses the idea of two opposites, equality, justice, and fairness—seeing both sides of a situation. Twos often seek balance and harmony and have great empathy for others.

Symbol: The line (two points joined together)

Astronomical body: The Moon

Day: Monday

Color: Green

Crystal: Emerald

Best days of the month for 2 as Life Path: 2nd, 11th, 20th

Character influences: Twos are inherently kind, with a high level of sensitivity to others. Twos thrive on social interaction and succeed professionally because they see both sides of a situation and make fair and honest assessments. In their personal lives, they may take on a challenging or unsuitable partner or friend because they prefer to see the best in people, even when this means they give more than they receive. They may avoid conflict and expend much time and energy healing others' hurts. Making friends and new contacts comes easily to a Two because they prioritize relationships and will always support and defend those they love.

Shadow character: Overgiving; giving too much weight to others' opinions; fearing judgment.

Advice: Trust your intuition rather than feeling obliged to others.

Number 3: The Triad—
Energy and Expression

Three was regarded as the perfect number by ancient philosophers. A symbol of fulfillment, the triangle was the subject of Pythagoras's famous theorem; he also taught that three expressed the nature of the universe as Matter, Idea, and God. Three is the number of energy, enthusiasm, optimism, and fulfillment. Threes are often dynamic, expressive character types.

Symbol: The triangle

Planets: Mars, Jupiter, or Mercury

Day: Tuesday

Color: Red

Crystals: Diamond, jasper

Best days of the month for 3 as Life Path: 3rd, 12th, 21st, 30th

Character influences: Threes prize creativity and freedom, and you organize your life accordingly—so you can pursue what truly fascinates you. This makes for a roller-coaster existence, riding high one minute and feeling lost the next, but the optimistic Three recovers quickly, begins again, and is often successful. You need stimulation and distraction, so regular nine-to-five office work may not suit you; you may prefer to travel for work or run your own projects or business. Threes are also great communicators and may excel at persuasion or direct selling, provided you believe in what you are offering.

Shadow character: Impulsiveness; overconfidence; impatience; lack of staying power.

Advice: Admit mistakes and see balance as a goal rather than a compromise.

Number 4: The Tetrad— Willpower and Order

Four was regarded as a symbol of truth in ancient times, and it denotes stability, structure, order, and willpower; it also signifies the four elements of Fire, Earth, Air, and Water. Fours are loyal and practical character types, who focus on creating lasting emotional and financial security.

Symbol: The square

Planet: Mercury or Uranus

Day: Wednesday

Colors: Blue, magenta

Crystals: Agate, topaz

Best days of the month for 4 as Life Path: 4th, 13th, 22nd, 31st

Character influences: Order is important to a Four type, so you prefer to follow rather than flout the rules and work in environments in which conventional structures are essential to achievement. At work and at home, you do not turn away from tough work and the jobs others will not do because you understand the value of these tasks in the greater scheme of supporting the whole. You may find fulfillment in spiritual service and enjoy being part of a large organization or network. Whatever your age, professional status, or time limitations, you do whatever needs to be done efficiently. Working as part of a team adds to your feeling of security. In relationships and friendships, Fours are outstandingly loyal and honest.

Shadow character: Lack of initiative; fussiness; martyrdom; difficulty adapting to new people or surroundings.

Advice: It's fine not to follow every rule; do things your way, too.

Number 5: The Pentad— Expansion and Freedom

Five is the number of vitality, discovery, and the five senses. Traditionally, the Pentad signified fertility and marriage, while the followers of Pythagoras also regarded five as a symbol of health. Five character types tend to be sensual, with great energy and curiosity.

Symbol: Pentagon, five-pointed star, or pyramid

Planet: Jupiter or Mercury

Day: Thursday

Color: Purple

Crystal: Red garnet

Best days of the month for 5 as Life Path : 5th, 14th, 23rd

Character influences: Fives are the ultimate multitaskers, who try many things; you may not succeed in every challenge you take on, but what counts is the adventure. You thrive on tests of courage and can be led by your heart. Fives may have many passionate affairs and often have lots of good friends, as you easily connect with others and are genuinely interested in their lives. In your professional life, you make a great strategist; perceptive and fast-acting, you know how best to respond to a problem or opportunity. Fives also have the ability to make the most of any situation and often appreciate the simpler things in life.

Shadow character: Casual thoughtlessness; lack of consideration; irresponsibility.

Advice: Bring your focus to one or two goals and consistently pursue them.

Number 6: The Hexad—Love and Protection

Six is the number of happiness, love, and idealism. It also denotes harmony, due to its geometric shape—the hexagon is perfectly balanced. Sixes are loving and seek a peaceful life. They aim to act for the higher good and are often sensitive and imaginative.

Symbol: The hexagon, the Seal of Solomon (two intersecting triangles)

Planet: Venus

Day: Friday

Colors: Yellow, pale blue

Crystals: Peridot, lapis lazuli

Best days of the month for 6 as Life Path: 6th, 15th, 24th

Character influences: The charitable Six enjoys giving to others and is motivated by love and the need for peaceful, caring relationships. If you have money, you are excited by what it can do to support those you love, how it might contribute to your community, and how it may help those who are less fortunate; wealth otherwise means little. This does not mean you are unambitious, however. You may be strongly motivated by creative projects, for example, but the goal is never financial. In relationships, you are loyal and caring, and you take your responsibility to others seriously.

Shadow character: Being too idealistic; neglecting good financial opportunities.

Advice: Avoid those who mistake your kindness for weakness.

Number 7: The Heptad— Mystery and Wisdom

Seven is the number of knowledge, self-discipline, mystery, and fate. It was regarded by Pythagoreans as special because it is the highest single-digit prime number. Sevens often have great wisdom and the resilience to stand by their ideas.

Symbol: The heptagon

Planet: Saturn or Neptune

Day: Saturday

Color: Gray

Crystal: Sapphire

Best days of the month for 7 as Life Path: 7th, 16th, 25th

Character influences: Sevens are associated with philosophy, wisdom, and imagination. Small concerns may not be of interest to you; your remit is the mysteries of this world and what is beyond. Intellectually ambitious, you may be ahead of your time. As a result, you become strong, enduring the pain of being rejected or misunderstood, but you know you can contribute to society through the knowledge you have acquired and have the determination to stand by your beliefs. You may be naturally reserved and recharge best in your own company.

Shadow character: Being overcritical; neglecting friendships; impracticality.

Advice: Focus on putting your knowledge into practice; manifest your ideas.

Number 8: The Ogdoad— Power and Success

Eight is the number of power in the material world. Mathematical philosophers regarded the Ogdoad as the first cube, denoting strength and reality. Eights are excellent organizers who achieve their goals.

Symbol: The cube (which has eight corners)

Planet: Uranus or Saturn

Day: Saturday

Color: Azure

Crystal: Amber

Best days of the month for 8 as Life Path: 8th, 17th, 26th

Character influences: Eights are practical, powerful, and determined to succeed; they often have a flair for business and are fast to react to an opportunity. Their focus is stability, but Eight character types can also embrace change because they respond brilliantly to it, reorganizing and adapting to create the security they value. They are kind and loving but tend not to fall in and out of love because this invites disruption; they prefer to nurture a deep, constant bond with a long-term partner. In friendships, they are giving and supportive but know where to draw the line if they feel they are being manipulated.

Shadow character: Being domineering; tactlessness; overly materialistic.

Advice: Listen to others' opinions; deepen your understanding.

Number 9: The Ennead— Spirituality and Courage

Nine is the number of intensity, courage, spirituality, genius, and boundaries. It is the last single-digit number before 10, said to hold the preceding numbers within itself. Nines are often inspired, highly intelligent people.

Symbol: The nonagon (nine-sided shape)

Planet: Neptune or Mars

Day: Thursday

Color: Lavender

Crystal: No specific crystal

Best days of the month for 9 as Life Path: 9th, 18th, 27th

Character influences: The Nine personality is similar to that of number Seven—both types are cerebral, but the Nine has the advantage of genius. As a Nine, you may be the ideal mentor, consultant, counselor, or adviser, and you have the potential to make an outstanding contribution to your field of work. Success comes due to your inspiring ideas and sharp intellect, so you may rise quickly in your chosen profession. The Nine has the gift of discernment and knows how and where to direct his or her energy and attention. You are a supportive, sympathetic, and loyal friend, just like the Six.

Shadow character: Lack of focus; inconsistency; inability to complete anything.

Advice: With sustained effort, anything is possible.

MASTER NUMBERS

Numbers 11 and 22 are believed to have intense vibrations. These types are often associated with having an evolved awareness.

Number 11: Intuition

Eleven can be considered a doubly empowered One. As 1s are associated with leadership, ingenuity, and communication, at the level of 11, the influence of the 1 expands into global communities and can also signify great faith. Elevens are believed to be visionary and charismatic individuals.

Planet: Neptune

Character influences: Eleven people often possess a special gift in a chosen subject area and a unique power of communication. You have the ability and drive to articulate your ideas, and you can passionately convince and motivate others. You have strong beliefs and values, and you'll often put a cause above your own needs, making personal sacrifices in order to help others. Some 11s are clairvoyants and healers and/or creative and artistic. You may feel a deep call to be of service to the world.

Shadow character: Overidentifying with a cause; lack of perspective; obsessiveness.

Advice: Temper your idealism so your goals remain realistic.

Number 22: Global Vision

Twenty-two is known as the number of the master builder. It comprises two Fours, the number of stability and structure, so whatever the Twenty-Two makes is designed to last. It may also be impressive, even a legacy for future generations. Twenty-Twos are therefore associated with power and the realization of a vision.

Planet: Uranus

Character influences: Twenty-Two people materialize ideas; whatever you envision, you make. It is important that you see results, so you may direct your energies into a physical product, building, or other environment that represents your values and beliefs. Equally, you may put together a group or evolve a larger organization or business that delivers a service or lasting benefit to others. Twenty-Twos are therefore highly sensitive to others' needs, with great empathy and compassion.

Shadow character: Stubbornness; lack of attention to important detail; intense anger.

Advice: Stay within reasonable boundaries; you don't need to push so hard.

YOUR PERSONAL YEAR AHEAD

Here's how to discover how you may fare in any year in the future.

First, add up your day and month of birth. Then add the year of your last birthday. Reduce all numbers, even 11 and 22, to a single digit and then see the interpretations below. The number you get is your personal year number until your next birthday. For example:

July 1, 2018

$7 + 1 + 2 + 0 + 1 + 8 = 19$

$1 + 9 = 10$

$1 + 0 = 1$

You're in a Year 1 until your birthday on July 1, 2019. After your birthday, you'll be in a Year 2 until your birthday on July 1, 2020, after which you'll be in a Year 3, and so on.

Year Numbers

YEAR 1: NEW BEGINNINGS

As Year 1 marks a new nine-year cycle, it offers new opportunities and beginnings. You're embarking on a new life phase, becoming the beginner as a student; following a new career path or starting a business or creative venture; or meeting a new partner or seeing new ways of relating in an established partnership. You may choose to change your look or take up a new interest. This is a year for innovation and dynamic, positive change. As the thrill of the new awakens, you feel ready to let go of old ties.

YEAR 2: RELATIONSHIPS AND DETAILS

This is a time for consolidating existing partnerships, friendships, and relationships with colleagues and clients. This may mean putting some relationships on a firmer footing and healing any past issues. A Year 2 means you are also primed to bring new contacts into your network and meet a new partner or friend, but the theme of the year, overall, is to work with what you have; pay close attention to existing professional and personal arrangements and look at the details of agreements to ensure they benefit you.

YEAR 3: EXPRESSION

A Year 3 makes all your effort worthwhile. It's time to express who you are. You'll find that ideas finally take shape in a way that is satisfying and joyful. Laughter and pleasure come naturally, as you express not only your vision, but your playful, creative side. While you enjoy the light, be prepared, too, to take your vision further; there are opportunities here for great personal development and achievement, from having a child to discovering a latent talent. Maximize every opportunity now, and you will continue to enjoy whatever you create beyond the Year 3 cycle.

YEAR 4: PRIORITIES

During Year 4, you'll be looking at ways to strengthen your position. With work and money, pay attention to finances and stay focused on your long-term goals. Your watchwords are effort, consistency, and efficiency, so break projects down into manageable stages to avoid burnout and protect long-term success. In love, Year 4 brings opportunities to resolve problems, bringing much-needed resolution—so you get closer or decide to go your separate ways.

YEAR 5: EXPLORATION AND CHANGE

Year 5 is a time of change and expansion as you delve into new possibilities. You may travel more or consider moving home, decide to learn a new skill, and/or expand your social networks as new people and places hold strong appeal. Year 5, however, does bring restlessness, along with a tendency to procrastinate; if you're overflowing with ideas, you will need to decide which are worth investigating. Overall, there is a freeing-up of energy as you test new boundaries. Certain truths may come to light, so you may decide to let go of a difficult love relationship and/or begin a new, lighthearted romance.

YEAR 6: LOVE

Love comes in all forms, from stronger family ties to romantic commitments. As you focus on your home life, you see what needs to get fixed—and who you need to forgive to move on. There's a fine balance between idealism and reality, however, so you may strive for perfection when it's unreasonable to expect it of yourself or others; conversely, you may overlook real faults or issues rather than confront them. Year 6, overall, is about how you create harmony; your emotional life takes priority.

YEAR 7: FOCUS ON THE SELF

Year 7 highlights the inner self and the subconscious. This is a time to nurture your needs rather than take on new responsibilities, as deeper issues are coming to the fore. As a result, you begin to question where you are in your life. Pay attention to your dreams and intuition and go slow: This is a time for contemplation and inspiration rather than dramatic change. In relationships, you may need more alone time to work through doubt or confusion. If stress has taken a toll on your health, create time for rest and healing.

YEAR 8: ACHIEVEMENT

To make the most of Year 8, reach out now; don't hide your talents, as this is a time of expansion and opportunity. A Year 8 is auspicious for beginning a new creative venture or business, which takes hard work and strategic thinking, but if you put in the effort, you will be recognized and rewarded. It's important to take charge in Year 8, however, as powerful energies abound; it could be tempting to go with the flow and give away too much of your time or money in your quest for success. In relationships, Year 8 can bring power struggles, but if you can resolve these, love deepens.

YEAR 9: COMPLETION AND REINVENTION

Year 9 brings endings and opportunities for renewal. You may find you're assessing your past achievements and relationships and sense that some situations, agreements, or relationships are coming to an end. If so, let it go; Year 9 brings natural endings, freeing up space so that you can move forward without regret. You may need to accept that not everything will fit to your schedule, however, so be prepared to allow events to unfold. Year 9 is auspicious for traveling and for deepening wisdom, giving you a greater sense of your identity and how you might contribute to the wider world.

SIGNIFICANT DAYS

Take the whole future date, then add it to your Life Path and Destiny numbers. You can use this technique when looking at potential start dates for a new job or any venture. For example, if you wanted to know if a future date would be good for a wedding, add up the date:

September 22, 2019

$9 + 2 + 2 + 2 + 0 + 1 + 9 = 25$

$2 + 5 = 7$

If, for example, your Life Path number was 5 and your Destiny number was 4, you would add the three numbers together: $7 + 5 + 4 = 16$. $1 + 6 = 7$.

A 7 is associated with the inner world rather than with togetherness or sociability. If you looked at September 21 instead, this gives a 6—the number of love and harmony, far more suited to a wedding.

Auspicious Numbers for Occasions	
Starting a new job, project, business	1, 8
Celebrations: weddings, parties	6, 3
Romantic dates	2, 6
Tests and examinations	7, 9
Compiling tax returns	4
Home remodeling	4
Travel	5, 9

NUMBER-DOWSING FOR A DAY

You can use a pendulum (see page 26) to dowse a "day" number, which offers a prediction for today. When you know the energy of the day, you can make the most of the influences and opportunities that arise. Take a pendulum and check your yes-no position. Hold the pendulum to stop any movement and then hold it above each number on your computer keyboard (or a row of numbers 1 to 9 on a piece of paper). Let the pendulum respond to each number and note those numbers that get a yes response. When you have finished, add up the numbers and reduce them to a single digit; then, refer to the year readings on pages 192 and 193 for your interpretation.

Numerology offers great insight into relationships. You will need your list of numbers, plus the full name and date of birth of your existing or potential mate. Calculate their numbers and compare them.

First, see if you have any common numbers and see where you differ. Experienced numerologists can offer detailed insights into compatibility, but you will get the feel of a relationship by comparing your digits. For example, if you had lots of 2s and 6s in your numerological makeup but your partner has 5s and 7s, this can say you value opposite things; you may be more sociable and peaceable, whereas your partner thrives on change and intellectual challenge. However, if your Soul numbers (calculated from the vowels in your names) were the same, this would suggest that there's a deep soul connection between you that could make this relationship work.

Differing numbers do not have to mean challenges, however. Your comparable numbers can also show what attracts you to a partner: Just look at the numbers in your list and see which are missing. If your partner has your missing numbers, this can reveal that you get certain needs met through them, as it's natural to seek out qualities in others that we lack (the same of course goes for friendships, too). If your partner

had 1s and 8s, which are not present in your numbers, your partner may be a high achiever at work, and you're attracted to the risk-taking aspect of his character.

A traditional list of harmonizing and conflicting numbers is below. Bear in mind that this is a broad interpretation, and that conflicting numbers do not have to be negatives; they can be lessons or growth opportunities. The numbers below show the people with whom you most naturally connect.

Number	Harmonizes with	Conflicts with
1	3 and 5	8
2	3 and 9	7
3	1, 2, 5, and 9	6
4	6, 7, and 8	5 and 9
5	1 and 3	4
6	4, 7, and 8	3
7	4 and 6	2
8	4 and 6	1
9	2 and 3	4

This number reveals the energetic qualities of an address based on the house or apartment number. See if your current abode supports you or if you are thinking of moving, calculate the number of a new potential address to see if it will be a good place for you to live.

Add together the digits of your house or apartment number to give a single digit from 1 to 9. For example: Apartment 307 would give 3 + 0 + 7 = 10, 1 + 0 = 1. If your address includes a letter, look up the number that corresponds to the letter on page 184. For an apartment 3a, you would take number 3 as the dominant energy and number 1 as the secondary energy or influence of that address. Read the meanings of both numbers below.

1 A 1 home is a lively, positive, and productive place, the perfect home for those working or running a business from home. One is the number of energy and independence, but you may miss that feeling of togetherness.

2 A 2 home is a gentle environment that supports peace. It's a good place for those who enjoy relaxed entertaining rather than impromptu get-togethers, as the number 2 represents balance.

3 A 3 home is great for music and parties and for those who express themselves creatively; Three signifies communication, so this home is the extrovert's paradise.

4 A 4 home is practical, with a good layout; it brings order and routine and can be an organized, efficient space. The number 4 denotes stability, so pay attention to this home's security.

5 A busy, creative hub, a 5 home supports innovation and free thinking. This is not the best match for those with more traditional values, as the number 5 signifies restlessness and seeking new experiences.

6 Six is the home number for comfort, family traditions, and teamwork; six is the number of harmony, so this is a good place for those seeking a sense of belonging in their wider community, too.

7 A 7 home brings protection and a sense of calm. It supports those who love to read or study, but as 7 is the number of the inner self and solitude, this is not a naturally sociable environment.

8 An 8 home makes an impression and suits people who have a reputation to uphold. This place suits confident people, as 8 is the number of opportunity and success, but those who are sensitive may feel the energy of this home is overwhelming.

9 People love to drop into a 9 home, as it is always welcoming and open to all. However, running a business from here may be fraught with distractions; Nine stands for boundaries, so a 9 home needs defined areas for work and home life.

THE MEANING OF YOUR PHONE NUMBER

Your phone number, a code via which you communicate daily, can influence the nature of its calls. By looking at the numerology of your phone number, you can see if the number you have generates the calls you want.

Take the number that you use most often—your cell phone number or a landline number at work, for example. See if you have any repeating digits and take a note of them, as these are a secondary influence. Add all the digits together, reduce them to a single number, and then see the interpretations below for your primary and secondary phone number meanings.

1 FACTS

When your number is 1, the calls you make or receive tend to be direct and to the point, and your authority and decisions are respected.

Good for: Entrepreneurs, self-employed people, those who work alone from home, and those who prefer not to engage in meandering chat.

2 LISTENING

You may be asked to resolve disputes, negotiate, or listen to friends' problems; the number is also associated with partnership and love. Two supports kindness, listening, and diplomacy, so is less suitable for those in high-pressure, deadline-oriented careers.

Good for: Caregivers, people-organizers, work involving direct contact with the public, and those who love a long conversation.

3 CREATIVITY

A 3 brings engaging, fun conversations and creative expression. This 3 also brings luck and is sometimes associated with fame and recognition, making your talents visible to the world. However, calls on a 3 can be open-ended, so may distract you from immediate goals.

Good for: Performers and communicators; creative discussions when there is no immediate deadline.

4 COMMITMENT

A 4 means the calls you receive may pressure you to be precise and committed and require you to be highly organized. However, a 4 can be restricting for free spirits who do not thrive on routine.

Good for: Accountancy, law, medicine, IT, and the caring professions.

5 INSPIRATION

With a 5, you may receive lots of calls from a variety of people; calls are stimulating but may be demanding. It's a good number for those who like to travel and socialize, but less so for those looking for commitment in love.

Good for: Freelance work, exploring ideas, selling.

6 LOVE, FAMILY, AND SHARING

With 6, you should get plenty of calls from loved ones, and these calls are long and chatty. The number is believed to attract love and romance but can also bring gossip.

Good for: Love, family, and friendship; also, community or teaching work.

7 DEEP CONNECTIONS

You may find you put off making and receiving calls because the timing of the call is not right. You may get intuitive flashes during calls, and when you do talk, the conversations are meaningful. This is not a sociable number but supports those with ingenious ideas.

Good for: Writers, healers, students, innovators, and those who need quiet time.

8 POWER

Eight is a powerful number that attracts success, money, loyalty, and self-confidence. However, while it supports those building material wealth, it is less harmonious for those on a spiritual path.

Good for: Business builders, managers, those with heavy responsibilities.

9 IDEALS

A conversation could go anywhere with a 9, as this number is associated with transformation; there's a global, humanitarian, or healing aspect here, too. Nine here is associated with luck but not necessarily great wealth.

Good for: Nonprofit organizations, charity work.

OTHER NUMBER DIVINATION METHODS

....

The two methods below reveal your future significant years and offer an answer to a burning question. While they may not be a part of today's numerological practices, they're fun to try.

The Vertical Number Formula: Significant Years

To find the years that hold special significance for you, write out your year of birth and then repeat it vertically. The years that come out of each calculation run from the past to the future. These years are not only significant, but can identify the beginning or end of a key life phase. For example, the years might include a year of marriage or the beginning of a committed relationship, a graduation, a new career direction, relocation, retirement, or a special achievement.

FOR EXAMPLE:

1972

1

9

7

2

1972 + 1 + 9 + 7 + 2 = 1991.

Repeat:

1991

1

9

9

1

1991 + 1 + 9 + 9 + 1 = 2011

And repeat again, until you have a year in the future:

2011

2

0

1

1

2011 + 2 + 0 + 1 + 1 = 2015

Then:

2015

2

0

1

5

2015 + 2 + 0 + 1 + 5 = 2023

The Pyramid of Fortune

This method looks complex, but it's a matter of simple adding up. You build the pyramid from the base, and the last number, at the tip of the pyramid, gives you your answer.

Write down your question in five words and then add up the number of letters in each word separately. The words can be any length, but the question must be five words because they will form the base of the pyramid. For example, if you asked, "Should I take this job?" You would have:

Should = 6   I = 1   Take = 4
This = 4   Job = 3

This gives the numbers 6, 1, 4, 4, 3. Write them as the bottom line of the pyramid:

6   1   4   4   3

To make the remaining lines, you add together the numbers that are next to each other. So, you would add 6 + 1 = 7, and then write the 7 in a new row above. The next row would be:

7   5   8   7
6   1   4   4   3

Continue for the next two lines, adding 7 + 5 = 12, which reduces to 3, and so on. Your next two rows will look like this:

7   1
3   4   6
7   5   8   7
6   1   4   4   3

The final number at the tip of the pyramid gives you the answer to your question, as shown below. Add 7 + 1 = 8.

8
7   1
3   4   6
7   5   8   7
6   1   4   4   3

See below for the interpretations. So, in answer to the question "Should I take this job?" the interpretation is 8: Are you really motivated to do this work? Also, this may not be a supportive environment for you, so consider carefully if this is your best move.

1   Success. Yes, in response to your question.

2   Failure. However, this may be due to lack of determination, so a positive outcome is possible, but only with effort and willpower.

3   Success, but to make the most of a yes, you will need to take action and be determined.

4   Some success, but a danger of failure; circumstances are not quite right at this time. Reflect on your question and use your own judgment.

5   A positive outcome, but this will take time. Be patient.

6   A positive outcome, provided you can think out a strategy. Success comes from thinking through an issue.

7   Success, provided your proposal or project is sound and meets with approval from others.

8   Failure due to lack of motivation on your part or lack of support from those around you. However, this can be reversed if you judge the situation carefully and rethink your position.

9   Success after a struggle, or in a form you do not expect.

Numbers can be spiritual messages; some view them as Angel Numbers, which offer guidance and reassurance (Angel Number meanings can differ from those in modern numerology). We often notice numbers when they repeat—for example, seeing number 11 in the time (10:11 a.m., 11:11 a.m.), as a phone number, on a car registration plate, or given in an appointment time (11 a.m.). We may also be sensitive to other number sequences, such as 1, 2, 3, or other recurring numbers; some people report noticing a number sequence two or three times a day. Numbers are all around us, constantly, from calories on a prepared food to page numbers in a book. We consciously notice a repeat pattern. We do not note every number that crosses our path, but when a number sequence or pattern occurs more than once, we give it significance; we sense it as a cosmic signal asking for attention.

11: Listen to your intuition; you are discovering your life purpose. New opportunities unfold.

22: Take the path of peace; find the right balance.

33: News concerning a creative project; Ascended Masters (evolved spiritual beings) offer guidance.

44: The number of the angels; keep working hard, as rewards will come. Your guardian angel is close by.

55: Change is coming; be free. Know that this is positive. An exciting new phase is about to begin.

66: Your angels support you. Follow your heart and spiritual knowing. Let go of financial worries.

77: Stay focused and rewards will come. You are about to achieve your goals.

88: Control your finances; your angels support you to get and stay organized and solvent. Eighty-eight can also signify karmic lessons.

99: A call to service that is your truth and life purpose.

1, 2, 3: Keep it simple; there's no need to complicate or overthink a situation.

1, 2, 3, 4, or other ascending sequences: Stay focused. You are going in the right direction.

201

DIVINATION
WITH
DICE

Dice for divination and gaming dates to ancient Egypt, classical Greece, and the countries of the Far East.

You will need three dice and a piece of paper and pen or a square of dark fabric and stick of chalk. First, mark a circle on your paper or fabric; make the diameter about the width of your palm. Next, allow a question to form. Shake the dice three times, thinking of your question. When you are ready, release the dice onto the cloth or paper.

Add up the numbers on the up-facing sides of all three dice, whether they fall within or outside the circle, and see below for the insight or answer to your question. It's believed that you will see the outcome of your question in nine days.

If any fall on the floor, this indicates disagreements. If the same number turns up more than once, this predicts great good luck coming your way. If any dice land one on top of another, the advice is to be cautious in your dealings with others; be skeptical and examine their motives carefully.

One die outside the circle: Regardless of the number interpretation, your goal can be achieved, but there will be challenges.

Two dice outside the circle: A difference of opinion affects the situation or goal.

Three dice outside the circle: You may get what you want, but it may not be in your best interests.

Three: Good luck is coming; sudden, positive developments.

Four: It's best not to follow this direction or line of thought.

Five: An unknown person can help you.

Six: There may be disappointment.

Seven: Small disagreements cause temporary disruption.

Eight: If you continue with this situation, there may be criticism from others.

Nine: Someone you know is getting married, and this may affect the situation you've inquired about.

Ten: Travel or distancing—and you may need to wait to see what impact this has. There may also be a birth that affects the outcome of your question.

Eleven: You may be apart from someone you love.

Twelve: You will find your answer in a letter that is coming soon.

Thirteen: An unwelcome outcome, if you pursue this.

Fourteen: A new friend will help you.

Fifteen: Be cautious to avoid trouble and opposition.

Sixteen: A journey brings happiness.

Seventeen: A situation gets complete, and this benefits you.

Eighteen: Immediate and great success that benefits everyone.

7

THE MYSTIC GAZE

SCRYING WITH CRYSTAL, WATER, AND MIRRORS

Scrying easily captures the imagination, yet we often step into divination through systems that offer known symbols. However, scrying can be immensely rewarding if we accept whatever we sense and receive. This is a challenge; after all, we believe we're supposed to physically "see" in reflective surfaces. But if we see a surface as a gateway to our inner eye, we discover a powerful technique for self-connection and divinatory knowing. Scrying can also heighten your visual and sensual awareness, benefiting other divination practices. You'll see more in a tea leaf star or tarot card as you make connections between image and meaning.

THE ORIGINS OF SCRYING

Gazing into crystal, liquid, or indeed any shiny surface for remote viewing, communication, and prophecy has enchanted people from many eras and cultures. Roman scryers, called *specularii*, searched for omens in the gleaming metal of a sword; the Huille-che tribe of Chile gazed into polished black stone; and Arabic boys divined with palmfuls of ink. John Dee, the sixteenth-century scholar-magician, possessed a "shew stone" for clairvoyance, while Nostradamus gazed at water and candle-flame to enter a trance-like state. All scrying materials hold the magical possibility that their reflective surfaces, through sight, touch, and technique, can potentially show us something beyond our own image.

We often take our first steps into divination work through systems that offer known symbols. Cards and runes give us marks and images. In teacup readings, the traces are already there, guiding us toward those intuitive leaps into interpretation. Yet scrying can be immensely rewarding—if we can turn our perception around and accept whatever we sense and receive, rather than anticipate fully formed, three-dimensional images. This can be tricky—after all, legend and other fictions have us believe that we're supposed to physically "see" in reflective surfaces. The queen in Snow White picks up her magic mirror, gazes within, and behold: a vision, clear and portent. In practice, however, the crystal or other object is a divination tool, just like dice, cards, or runes. If we see a surface as a way to spark intuition rather than a mirror in which we expect to see literal images, we discover a powerful technique for self-connection and divinatory knowing.

HOW SCRYING WORKS

The English astrologer Edward Lyndoe suggested in the 1930s that scrying works due to the iron content of the materials used. It was believed that iron attracted emanations from the spiritual realm, which were transmitted to us through the iron in the body; so the iron content within us and the iron in the material set up a resonance with the spiritual world.

Here's another potential explanation: Scrying gives our logical left brain a physical object to focus on while the intuitive right brain can get to work, without the left brain jumping in to judge or block intuitive responses. Meditating on an object creates a change in consciousness; we shift from our everyday reality into the imaginal, intuitive realm. We might sense or directly see colors or shapes, and because we're in that meditative zone, we can interpret what we see widely.

A shape might be a symbol of a situation, a metaphor for how we live, or a literal prediction. For example, an airplane would indicate a journey; a butterfly might suggest a butterfly state of mind or, alternatively, fleeting happiness; and an anchor might indicate security—or being tied down. An image does not have to be defined to be important, so pay attention to cloudy, vague shapes, too. As you gaze (and blink whenever you need to), you may just find that an image develops on the surface or you see with your inner vision, receiving an image in your mind.

Scrying works when we set a positive intention to receive and work for the highest good. Approach your crystal, candle, or water with an open attitude, and you will discover it has much to say.

WHEN TO SCRY

There are several timing traditions, but overall, be guided by that pull of anticipation: whenever you sense a question building and feel that it is time to ask. If you feel connected with the moon, you can also choose a time when the moon is increasing (waxing), as this represents a situation or energy growing, rather than during a waning moon, which is a time of decreasing energy. One tradition suggests you begin a scrying session just before twilight, which is associated with occult manifestations. If you are crystal-gazing, you can choose the day of the week that is associated with your crystal ball or slab (see opposite).

TIMING AND RECORDING YOUR SESSIONS

Begin by timing yourself for one minute, then three, then five. When you begin, scrying can feel intense, so set a timer to limit your sessions. As you become more comfortable, build up to five minutes or longer if it feels right. It is also helpful to do your mystic gazing in the same place and at the same time each day, as this helps build connection with your crystals or ritual.

After a session, journal what you experienced or draw what you saw or sensed, and review it as events unfold.

CRYSTAL BALL READING: CRYSTALLOMANCY

Crystallomancy means "divination by crystals." Crystal balls have been used for divination for centuries, to the extent that the crystal ball has become the symbol of the psychic or clairvoyant reader; an image of a crystal ball instantly says "divination" or "future."

You can work with any size ball. Crystals with inclusions and clouds are perfect, as the light we use to read with illuminates these features, creating a fantastical stage for our intuition.

The crystals listed here are those associated with crystal-gazing, but you can choose any crystal ball or flat crystal with which you sense a connection. Also listed are the associations with these crystals, along with their day of the week. For example, if you had an amethyst crystal ball, you might want to scry with it on a Thursday to further activate its ability to connect you with the spiritual realms.

Crystals and Their Divinatory Qualities

Crystal	Helps activate
Amethyst	Spiritual connection; psychic ability
Aquamarine	Spiritual connection; perspective
Citrine	Intuition; manifesting
Clear quartz	Clarity; spiritual connection; manifesting
Fairy quartz	Faery connection; practical guidance
Labradorite	Intuition; psychic ability
Lemurian quartz	Angelic connection; oneness; accessing ancient wisdom
Obsidian	Spiritual growth; past lives
Rose quartz	Love and relationships; compassion
Rutilated quartz	Channeling; manifesting
Selenite	Angelic connection; stability
Smoky quartz	Groundedness; patience

Crystals and the Days of the Week

Day	Crystal
Monday	Selenite
Tuesday	Clear quartz
Wednesday	Citrine
Thursday	Amethyst, aquamarine
Friday	Rose quartz
Saturday	Obsidian, labradorite
Sunday	Rutilated quartz

PREPARATION: MAKING A CONNECTION

You will need a crystal ball, some dark cloth or a dark surface, a candle, and a notebook or paper. Choose a candle that is shorter than your crystal ball so the light or flame you use will shine through most of the crystal (you'll set your light behind your crystal ball). If you have a small ball, for example, a tealight would be suitable (and you can also use electric tealights or candles; you don't need a naked flame). Whatever size ball you have, you can try the flashlight app on your smartphone. Keep the notebook or paper and pen to hand because you might prefer to jot down impressions during your gazing session for reflection later.

Cleanse your crystal ball by bathing it in moonlight for several consecutive nights or using one of the methods listed on page 16. Do not cleanse it by placing it in direct sunlight, as this poses a fire hazard.

1 You'll need to work in a quiet room with subdued lighting (bright sunlight or bright indoor lighting creates reflections on the crystal's surface). Lower or turn off the lights.

Sit comfortably and set your intention; holding your crystal, take a breath and ask it to work with you for your higher good. Ask, also, for any necessary protection during the reading; you can visualize yourself in a bubble of white light. This traditional protection method guards against any negative influences and is particularly important when scrying with old mirrors (see page 217).

2 Keep holding your crystal ball, sensing a growing connection between you and your crystal. Close your eyes and see what you sense, feel, and see. It's important to do this, particularly if you are a beginner; looking directly into a crystal without preparation can in some cases block the intuitive pathway because the expectation that we should immediately "see" an image sets up resistance to openness.

3 Now, open your eyes and, still holding your crystal, gaze into its surface; visualize the crystal taking you on a journey. Sense the vibration of the crystal in your hands and allow any sensations to arise without asking a question. Tune in to your senses: You might get flashes of color; sensations in your body, such as a light tingling; or you may simply feel peaceful. Take at least five minutes just to be with your crystal in this way, opening up a channel of communication between you.

HOW TO BEGIN SCRYING

1 Place your crystal ball on its stand, light a candle or switch on your tealight or flashlight app, and place the light source behind the crystal ball. Move the light around, still behind the ball, until the position feels right. You may begin to see images forming and changing as you move the light. Areas that appeared cloudy without illumination now begin to have depth. Slowly turn the ball around on its stand; again, you will see the crystal landscape change. Let the ball rest in the position that you sense is right to begin; you can continue to move the crystal and light source throughout the reading.

2 When you are ready, consider your question. You may prefer to ask the crystal for insights into a situation or for general guidance. Speak your question aloud or silently up to three times and then gaze into your crystal. You can do this:

• With your eyes open.

• With your eyes half-shut, so the crystal becomes soft-focus.

• With your eyes closed; you may find that you naturally close your eyes and see mental images.

Stay relaxed and don't consciously try to see. Blink whenever you need to, rather than fix a stare. Find a focal point within the crystal: This might be an inclusion, a spot where light refracts, a tiny fracture within the crystal, or a cloudy area. Keep your breathing slow and steady. If any extraneous thoughts distract you, just observe them and let them go, returning to your focal point. The more relaxed you feel, the easier it is for you to recognize images and sense messages.

WHAT DO YOU SEE? THE MEANINGS OF SYMBOLS AND COLORS

Symbols are traditionally said to appear on the right of the crystal ball, but they can appear anywhere (and you may receive them in your mind rather than through an image on the ball). Here are some conventional interpretations:

Rising clouds: Yes in answer to a question.

Descending clouds: No.

Waning moon (a C-shape): Decrease and possible loss.

Waxing moon (a mirror-image C): Growth and prosperity.

Heart: Love.

Ship or plane: Travel.

For other symbols, use the list of tea leaf symbols (see page 74). Above all, interpret any symbols you see in your own way. You may also find you hear messages rather than literally see colors and symbols; if you do, write them down.

Take note of any colors you see. The traditional meaning of colors in scrying are as follows, but you may have your own.

Red: Danger.

Orange: Anger.

Yellow: Challenges.

White: Positive energy, protection.

Blue: Success.

Green: Happiness, health.

Black and gray: Negative energy.

Light shades of any color apart from gray—pink, lemon, or lilac, for example—are considered positive. Overall, though, interpret the colors in terms of how you respond to them, rather than adhere to standard color interpretations.

You may hear words during scrying. Some practitioners do not see images but get names or messages; others experience bilocation, the feeling of being in two places at once.

ENDING THE SESSION

When you have finished scrying, thank the crystal for its messages, take a breath, and bring yourself back to the present moment. Wrap your crystal in dark cloth and place it in a safe place, away from light, to protect its energy. Extinguish or turn off the candle.

WATER-GAZING: HYDROMANCY

Hydromancy means divination by water; a bowl of water becomes a vessel for images and other divinatory signs. Water is a medium of communication, a river of the collective unconscious through which we psychically connect.

Water-gazing is practiced indoors, using a bowl of water, or outdoors, by observing water features such as streams, pools, or lakes. Any colors or images seen in the water are interpreted in response to a request or specific question.

Water-gazing needs patience and time; one of the simplest ways to establish a connection with water as a means of divination is by observing the interaction of air with water. The appearance of ripples or bubbles on the water's surface were interpreted as yes answers when water-gazing was practiced in ancient Persia. Paying close attention to changes in the surface of water is great preparation for water-scrying, as you are asked only to observe what is physically present in the water, without pressure to see anything more. When you are comfortable with this, you will find that you begin to connect with the energy of the water and naturally begin to sense images and symbols as your awareness expands.

This basic water-gazing technique requires just a bowl of water, a crystal, and a candle.

Prepare the room and set your intention for your reading (see "Preparation," on page 210). Use a medium bowl, black or another dark color; avoid bowls that are patterned on the inside, as this can interfere with the images you may see. (If you don't have a dark or black bowl, use a white bowl and scry with cooled black tea.) Fill it with water until it is around half full; this can be right from the tap, or you can use bottled spring water that you dedicate specifically to water-scrying and reuse each time. Place a quartz crystal or amethyst in the bottom of the bowl. The white or clear quartz and the amethyst represent spiritual connection and intuition; the stone also gives you a focal point during scrying. Light a candle, placing it near the bowl so it casts a little light on the water.

1 Take a breath and formulate a question. You might ask what will happen in the future or simply ask if there is anything you need to see at this moment.

2 Begin by focusing on the crystal and seeing what appears in the water around it. This helps you enter a relaxed but focused mindset. You might half-close your eyes or feel you need to close your eyes and see with your inner eye. If you discern an image, take a mental note and continue gazing until you sense a withdrawal of energy and feel ready to stop. Take a breath and come back to the present moment and then write down or draw your impressions. Consider what they represent for you (or refer to the symbols for tea leaf readings on page 74, or any dream dictionary).

ALTERNATIVE METHODS:
DYES AND OIL

Rather than place a crystal in the bowl, use a transparent bowl and add a few drops of food coloring. The dye tracks the currents of the water and forms shapes or patterns that you can interpret. You can also drip some oil (cooking oil is fine) onto the water surface and see what images form as it moves over the surface.

THE MOON OVER WATER

The moon has a natural affinity with water and with divination, as the moon is associated with unconscious knowing; it connects with the subtle light within us. This practice takes place on a night of a full moon, which represents fullness and enlightenment (perfect when you need an enlightened answer to a question). Take a bowl of water outside on the night of a full moon and set it so the moon is fully reflected in the water. Sit or stand so you can see the reflection, take a breath, set your intention, and gaze into the water, using the moon as a focal point.

CANDLE READINGS: CEROMANCY

Ceromancy means "candle divination." It encompasses interpreting the quality of a candle flame, how a candle burns, smoke patterns, and candle wax readings.

CANDLE FLAME DIVINATION

How the candle burns and the appearance of the flame are taken as a response to your question. This technique is about literal observation rather than scrying the flame for images and signs.

Set up a candle in a holder in a still, quiet space. Keep the candle away from drafts, as this can affect how it burns. Place the candle so it is within arm's reach; if it is too close to you, your breathing may affect the flame's movement (and may not be safe). As you light the wick, take a deep breath, exhale, and ask your question. Now watch the flame for a minute or so and interpret it as follows:

A bright, steady flame: The way ahead is clear. There are no obstacles to your wish.

A small flame, weak flame, and/or a flame that goes out: Is this the right path for you (or the right question)? Blocks and opposition.

Jumping flame: An intense, volatile situation. Consider if you are willing to continue or take another direction.

Flickering flame: Commitment issues.

Hissing flame: A message from spirit is coming to you. News.

Smoking flame: Any negativity in your life is being cleared. New opportunities await.

SMOKE DIVINATION

While divining patterns made by candle smoke is often written about, it's virtually impossible to do without setting fire to the piece of paper you use. It may work for you safely if your candle gives out a lot of smoke, so you can keep the paper an inch or two away from the flame, but this does take practice. Here, we use an incense stick rather than a candle. You will still need to guard against the paper catching fire, so do this by a bowl of water or a sink.

Prepare a slim incense stick and a piece of white paper. Before you begin, it's worth experimenting with a spare piece of paper to find the right distance between the paper and flame—you want the smoke to mark the paper, but not to burn it. When you are ready to begin, take a breath, think of your question or request, and light the incense stick. Allow the flame to burn, rather than blowing it out so the stick smolders, as you usually would. Next, quickly move the piece of paper above the tip of the flame three times. Extinguish the flame and examine the paper. What shapes do you see in the smoke marks? For example, in response to her question "What do I need to know about work coming my way?" Shona saw the V-shape of bird wings and a curved body and beak, like a flying swan. She interpreted this as financial benefits coming through work (see the tea leaf symbol meanings, page 74).

CANDLE-WAX DIVINATION

For a wax reading, you will need water, any type of candle, and a bowl or pan. Don't use your best china, as you'll be adding wax to the water. If you're using a white candle, use a black or dark-colored bowl to make the wax more visible.

Fill your pan or bowl with tap water. Set your intention for your candle-wax reading. Light the candle and let it burn down for a minute or two to give enough wax to drip into the water. Meanwhile, think of your question. Now, swirl the water around with a spoon and then remove the spoon and drip some candle wax into the swirling water.

What do you see? Look at what is emerging from the solidifying wax. If you make out a symbol or number, for example, consider what this represents for you (or look at the list of tea leaf symbols and number meanings starting on page 74.) If you asked a yes or no question and you like the images you see, the answer to your question is yes.

ALTERNATIVE METHOD: SCRYING WITH EGG WHITE

If you do not have a candle, try scrying with egg white; this is known as oomancy, or egg divination. Prepare a bowl of hot water and hold the egg in both palms, thinking of a question or asking generally for guidance or a prediction. When you are ready, stir the water with a spoon and crack the egg, separating the white from the yolk by tipping the yolk from one part of the shell into the other so the egg white drips into the water. Set the yolk and shell parts aside and gaze into the water as the shapes from the egg white take form.

SCRYING WITH MIRRORS:
CATOPTROMANCY

John Dee's shew stone.

Catoptromancy, or mirror divination, is an ancient technique that we have access to every day. You can use a black mirror, a switched-off laptop screen, or a regular mirror to become catoptromancy adept.

The black mirror, or "magic mirror," is a disk of polished obsidian that was used for divination in the Aztec period. The Elizabethan scholar and astrologer Dr. John Dee owned one, believed to have come from a statue of Aztec god Tezcatlipoca, whose name means "smoking mirror." Dee used his mirror, or "shew stone," to connect with the angelic and spirit realms through trance medium Edward Kelly; both men gazed into the rich black obsidian glass as Dee asked questions and Kelly relayed the answers.

You can make your own black mirror using a glass picture frame. Remove the frame and any backing paper or card, clean the glass, and cleanse it by visualizing white light running over the surface from left to right. Paint one side with several coats of black acrylic paint, which gives a matte finish, and let it dry. Put it back in the frame so the reflective, unpainted side is faceup.

Whether you choose a black mirror, a desktop or laptop computer screen, or a regular mirror, there are two ways to scry. Experiment with both to see which suits you best:

- Sit before the mirror or screen so you're reflected in it. As you look at your reflection, you may find your image begins to change and you begin to see your face transform into different shapes and forms, or these shapes and forms emerge in the space around your face.

- Sit with the screen or mirror at an angle, so you are not reflected in the mirror, but you still have full view of it.

SCREEN-SCRYING

Switch off the computer. Clean the screen with a soft cloth or screen wipe. Set the intention to cleanse it before you begin: You can also visualize white light passing over it from left to right. Take two candles and set them up at each side of the screen. Turn off the lights in the room, close the blinds, and close the door to minimize all other light sources. Sit in front of the screen or at an angle.

1 Take a deep breath, close your eyes, and allow a question to form in your mind. If you don't have a specific question, set the intention to receive a message through words, colors, or symbols.

2 Half-open your eyes and gaze into the screen. Relax, breathe, and visualize that you are opening to receive any impressions that arise. Look beyond your own reflection.

Trust yourself and your experience. You may sense a color or the outline of a form in your peripheral vision; sometimes, an image forms on the screen or in your mind. Consider what that image or color means for you (see also the interpretations for tea leaf readings starting on page 74, or dream dictionary symbols). For example, you may see the outline of someone you know or knew or a significant symbol: Stars might mean success for you, or horses might mean affection.

Extinguish the candles when the session is over.

ALTERNATIVE METHOD: THE REGULAR MIRROR

To use a regular mirror, find a dark room with no other reflective surfaces (such as wall mirrors) in it. It's believed that old mirrors work best, possibly because they have residual energetic imprints. Follow the method above, lighting two candles in a dark room, and remember to envelop yourself in white light for protection; as old mirrors often carry the residue of their past owners, it is important to protect yourself from any negative imprints.

RECORD YOUR READINGS

DATE   INSIGHTS

BIBLIOGRAPHY

Runes

Aswynn, Freya. *Power and Principles of the Runes*. Thoth Publications, 2007.

Bellows, Henry Adams. *The Poetic Edda*. Princeton University Press, 1936.

Church, Alfred John, and William Jackson Brodribb, trans. *The Works of Tacitus*. Modern Library, 2003.

Dee, Jonathan. *Runes: Reading, Casting, and Divination*. Kerswell Farm Ltd., 2007.

Crystal divination

Clark, Charles Upson. *The Text Tradition of Ammianus Marcellinus*. New Haven, 1904.

Eason, Cassandra. *A Complete Guide to Divination*. Piatkus, 1998.

Smith, Adam T., and Jeffrey F. Leon. "Divination and Sovereignty: The Late Bronze Age Shrines at Gegharot, Armenia." *American Journal of Archaeology* 118, no. 4 (October 2014): 549–63.

Tea leaf reading

Fenton, Sasha. *Tea Cup Reading: Tasseography*. Zambezi Publishing, Ltd, 2000.

Palmistry

Barrett, David V. *Palmistry*. Dorling Kindersley, 1995.

Cheiro (Count Louis Hamon). *Cheiro's Language of the Hand*. Arrow Books, 1986.

Heron-Allen, Edward. *Palmistry: A Manual of Cheirosophy*. Read Books, 2013; first published 1887.

Playing cards

Dee, Jonathan. *Fortune Telling with Playing Cards*. Zambezi Publishing, Ltd, 2004.

Foli, Professor P. R. S. *Fortune Telling by Cards*. C. Arthur Pearson, 1906.

Platt, Charles. *Card Fortune-Telling*. W. Foulsham & Co., LTD., 1878.

Sepharial. *The Art of Card Fortune Telling*. Kessinger Publishing, 2010.

Waite, A. E. *A Manual of Cartomancy and Occult Divination*. Kessinger Publishing, 2010; first published 1909.

Tarot cards

Dean, Liz. *The Ultimate Guide to Tarot*. Fair Winds Press, 2015.

Dean, Liz. *The Mystery of the Tarot*. CICO Books, 2003.

Decker, Depaulis, and Dummett. *A Wicked Pack of Cards*. Duckworth, 2002.

Numerology

Moorey, Teresa. *The Numerology Bible*. Godsfield Press, 2012.

ABOUT THE AUTHOR

Liz Dean is a tarot teacher and professional tarot reader at Psychic Sisters within Selfridges, London. A former commissioning editor in illustrated book publishing, Liz is the author of fourteen books and card decks, including HBO's *Game of Thrones Tarot*, *The Ultimate Guide to Tarot*, *The Ultimate Guide to Tarot Spreads*, *The Art of Tarot*, *Fairy Tale Fortune Cards*, *The Victorian Steampunk Tarot*, and *Switchwords: How to Use One Word to Get What You Want*. She is a former coeditor of *Kindred Spirit*, the United Kingdom's leading spiritual magazine. Her work has been featured in the national UK press, including *Spirit & Destiny* and the *Daily Express*.

www.lizdean.info

www.switchwordspower.com

INDEX

222

223

224